AF483239

# Living in Darkness

Scott Barnes

ISBN:

# Dedication

This book is dedicated to my loving family and for love of country and or devotion to one's country, who have been my pillars of strength and support throughout this journey.

To my mother, whose unwavering encouragement and belief in my dreams have inspired me to pursue my passion for writing and her endless patience, understanding, and her unwavering love, even during the late nights and early mornings spent lost in the world of words.

Thank you for being my constant source of inspiration and for walking alongside me on this adventure.

This book is for you

# Acknowledgment

I'd like to thank everyone who played a significant role in bringing this book to fruition. Your support and encouragement have been invaluable throughout this journey.

Special thanks to [Phyllis Burns] for her support, and Randall Barnes for his support.

I am grateful to my family and friends for their unwavering support and understanding during the long hours spent in writing and editing. Your belief in me fueled my determination.

A sincere thank you to Google and Amazon KDP for believing in this project and providing a platform for its publication.

Lastly, to the readers who embark on this literary adventure, your interest in my work is the ultimate reward.

Thank you all for being part of this incredible experience.

- Scott Barnes

# CONTENTS

# About The Author

Scott Barnes is an accomplished author, known for his captivating storytelling and compelling narratives. With a passion for literature that began in childhood, Scott has always been drawn to the power of words to transport readers to new worlds and ignite their imagination.

Born and raised in a small town, Scott's love for writing blossomed early on. He spent countless hours immersed in books, crafting his own stories and dreaming of one day sharing them with the world. Scott embarked on a journey to pursue his dreams of becoming a published author.

Scott has continued to captivate readers throughout his career with his unique voice and masterful storytelling. His works span various genres, from mystery to children's books, each one drawing readers in with its depth and complexity.

With a talent for crafting unforgettable stories that resonate with readers long after the final page is turned, Scott Barnes continues to enchant audiences with his literary works, leaving an indelible mark on the world of literature.

Historical Fiction with mystery and children's books.

Page Blank Intentionally

# The Sixties

His neighbor recalls the young child five years of age, in 1964, living in Fox Chase. The people who resided in the neighborhood were hard-working people who wanted to get away from the city. The house was an old, dilapidated, drafty, wooden house with coal heat and a dark, cold basement for shoveling coal for heat into a furnace. The front yard was dirt. This house was one of few left with coal heat, built before gas heat came out.

There would be a truck that would come around and put a wooden shoot in your basement window and dump it on the floor. Coal heat was one of the first home heating options; Gas didn't come out until later. But it was available, Blake said; it was piped in with new construction.

At an early age he started feeling a distance from his father or started to feel no connection. When he would come home drunk and yell and tell him to get a beer out of the refrigerator, it furthered a further distance when Blake was always told to shovel the coal in the coal stove. It was a damp basement with little light. You opened the door of the stove and shoveled coal inside.

They lived on Rhawn Street in Philadelphia, Pennsylvania. They were actually living there for some years, perhaps up to 5 years of age, with an older sister and two younger brothers and a mother and father. Blake was born in a Montgomery County hospital. There is no such thing as a bad child at an early age. Some people try to communicate and lead with guidance, and others have issues of personal arguments that don't have time for their children, such as drinking and survival. And at times, we didn't get food.

Money or poverty is always an issue to communicate with children unless the parents sway their thinking. A lot of times, it turns into a Single parent situation. You have one parent who drinks, and the other one doesn't. The inevitable was on its way. Know there is a challenge of a one parent situation that puts you in a lower income. And you are classified as a community problem. There was no such thing as Church help and community or Welfare.

There was a rumor that John F Kennedy was assassinated. His initials and his nickname often referred to JFK. Jack was the 35 president and American politician of the United States from 1960 to 1963. He was a Navy man and a Democrat who proposed to abolish the Electoral College. There were rumors that he had affairs with hookers and an actress. Supposedly, the Mafia was giving him women to try and get their grips on him. He dated a Communist spy and she was passing on information.

He was under investigation by the F.B.I. for not only Mafia ties but also Russian ties. The theories were flying around. There was wiretapping on the Teamsters Union and also an actress. J.F.K. was dating her, and she took sleeping pills that killed her. And perhaps she was dead 4 hours before, and her body was moved. It led to questions of a crime that may have been covered up. Kennedy had stopped by and saw her? Was there a Liaison?

There are some theories about who killed him, but there was a name from an intelligence source, Blake can't recall, who really had him killed in Dallas, Texas, in his motorcade. He was running to promote his next campaign and decided to go to Texas. There's hidden evidence that he got shot three times? It was talked about for years. There were rumors his Grandfather was a booze runner and his father was a Banker, one of the wealthiest men in the world, and that started the dynasty.

The blue-collar workers of America are part of the backbone of American production and innovation in the advancement of Agriculture, Manufacturing, and Business. People's Relatives came to America for work, and they worked hard to make an honest living. There were generations of Police Officers in Fox Chase who worked in different departments that worked in the hard-core neighborhoods.

The Fox Chase train station line, was about 20 feet from the house and branched from the mainline to Newtown and the city. The line of Newtown opened up in 1878 to Newtown and Center City, Philadelphia.

They tried to go to New York City but failed. It mainly runs through the city and connects with some suburban stations. And it has cut ties with Montgomery County and it's not in their future. However, it was more of a picturesque place. Fox Chase was on the outskirts of the city of Philadelphia.

The train station went a little further, perhaps to Lower Moreland for a time. However, with the Fox Chase Train station there, you can navigate through the country. At the time you could walk around the corner there were a few stores and a sandwich shop. There was a bar across the street up the street and around the corner.

There was a park nearby, it was called, Burholme Park, with a mansion that was built in 1859. A wealthy importer of goods and a president of the Tioga railroad to be the family's summer home. It was a farm for horses, and later on, it became an animal rights activist place. It was a Farm that was for the Aged Equines.

The mansion was later turned into a Library with a parking lot. It has a driving range and a miniature golf course below, with trees around it with a baseball field.

Fox Chase was a dispute between two different townships next to one another, Montgomery County and Philadelphia, that gained a lot of support from 1916 to 1923. The close local identification with Fox Chase was the strength of this movement. A petition to the county Court of Quarter sessions was initiated. After the court's rejection, the movement was abandoned because the Borough residents had second thoughts due to Philadelphia's Taxes and schooling. The Philadelphian elite was building vacation homes in Fox Chase a hundred years ago.

In the landscape, there are wetlands, woodlands, and meadows, and trails. A park called Penny Pack bordering the city. The area's character changed with the arrival of the Railroad in 1876, which was expanding throughout the country.

Fox Chase farm is perhaps the only remaining farm in the county and is used for school districts. It began in 1822 as a land grant from William Penn to Lord Stanley and then passed on to another family for over 200 years. Now, people take care of it as a pastoral treasure. The volunteer groups currently assist in maintaining and preserving the pastoral treasure for present and future generations.

William Penn was a Quaker who owned the State of Pennsylvania. The Quakers belonged to the Religious Society of Friends, a historically Protestant Christian set of denominations. A belief generally unites members of these movements in each human's ability to experience the light within or "Answer that of God in everyone" Some profess a priesthood of all believers inspired by the First Epistle of Peter. They include those with evangelical, holiness, and traditional Quaker understandings of Christianity. There are also Non-theist Quakers whose spiritual practice does not rely on the existence of God. To differing extents, the Friends avoid creeds and hierarchical structures.

Some 89% of Quakers worldwide belong to evangelical and programmed branches that hold services with singing and a prepared Bible message coordinated by a pastor. Some 11% practice waiting for worship or un-programmed worship (Commonly Meeting for Worship,) where the unplanned order of service is mainly silent and may include unprepared vocal ministry from those present. Some meetings of both types have Recorded Ministers present, Friends recognized for their gift of vocal ministry.

The proto-evangelical Christian movement dubbed Quakerism arose in mid-17th-century England from dissenting Protestant groups breaking with the established Church of England. The Quakers, especially the Valiant Sixty, sought to convert others by traveling through Britain and overseas preaching the Gospel. Some early Quaker ministers were women. They based their message on a belief that "Christ has come to teach his people himself," stressing direct relations with God through Jesus Christ and faith in the universal priesthood of all believers. This personal religious experience of Christ was acquired by direct experience and by reading and studying the Bible. Quakers focused their private lives on behavior and speech reflecting emotional purity and the light of God, with a goal of Christian perfection.

Although born into a distinguished Anglican family and the son of Admiral Sir William Penn, Penn joined the Religious Society of Friends or Quakers at the age of 22. The Quakers obeyed their "Inner light" which they believed to come directly from God. Penn was a close friend of George Fox, the founder of the Quakers. These were times of turmoil, just after Cromwell's death, and the Quakers were a suspect because of their principles, which differed from the state-imposed religion, and because they refused to swear an oath of loyalty to Cromwell or the King (Quakers obeyed the command of Christ not to swear, Matthew 5:34.)

Penn's religious views were highly distressing to his father, Admiral Sir William Penn. His father earned an estate in Ireland and hoped that Penn's charisma and intelligence would be able to win him favor at the court of Charles II. He was imprisoned for writing a tract (The Sandy Foundation Shaken) which attacked the doctrine of the Trinity.

"If thou wouldst rule well, thou must rule for God, and to do that, thou must be ruled by him. Those who are not governed by God will be ruled by tyrants". –William Penn

Penn was a frequent companion of George Fox, the founder of the Quakers, travelling in Europe and England with him in their ministry.

He also wrote a comprehensive, detailed explanation of Quakerism, along with a testimony to the character of George Fox, in his Introduction to the Autobiographical Journal of George Fox.

Penn was educated at Essex where he had his earliest religious experience. After that, young Penn's religious views effectively exiled him from English society — he was sent down (expelled) from Christ Church, Oxford, for being a Quaker and was arrested several times. Among the most famous of these was the trial following his arrest with William Meade for preaching before a Quaker gathering. Penn pleaded for his right to see a copy of the charges laid against him and the laws he had supposedly broken, but the judge, the Lord Mayor of London, refused — even though the law guaranteed this right. Despite heavy pressure from the Lord Mayor to convict the men, the jury returned a verdict of "Not guilty" The Lord Mayor then not only had Penn sent to jail again (on a charge of contempt of court) but also the full jury. The members of the jury, fighting their case from prison, managed to win the right for all English juries to be free from the control of judges. The persecution of Quakers became so fierce that Penn decided that it would be better to try to find a new, free Quaker settlement in North America. Some Quakers had already moved to North America, but the New England Puritans, especially, were as hostile towards Quakers as the people back home, and some of them had been banished to the Caribbean.

He founded Pennsylvania in 1677. Penn's chance came as a group of prominent Quakers, among them Penn, received the colonial province of West New Jersey (half of the current state of New Jersey, Delaware, and Maryland. He also participated in forming the thirteen colonies. That same year, two hundred settlers from the towns of Chorleywood and Rickmansworth in Hertfordshire and other towns in nearby Buckinghamshire arrived and founded the town of Burlington. Penn, who was involved in the project but himself remained in England, drafted a charter of liberties for the settlement. He was for a fair trial by jury, freedom of religion, and speech. He was also against slavery. However, it was unlikely because he had some. His Friends had enormous amounts of land all over. This was the beginning of forming The Thirteen Colonies. Later on, the thirteen colonies are made: Connecticut, Delaware, Georgia, Maryland, Massachusetts, New Hampshire, New Jersey, New York, North Carolina, Pennsylvania, Rhode Island, South Carolina, and Virginia.

The American Revolutionary War was on its way. It began on (April 19, 1775 – and September 3, 1783), also known as the War of Independence; it was the military conflict of the American Revolution in which American Patriots who also fought alongside with Militia forces largely under George Washington's command and defeated the British and or The King from England, from collecting Taxes, and Religious Freedom, and Independence resulting in the Treaty of Paris (1783) recognizing the independence and sovereignty of the United States.

Fighting began on April 19, 1775, at the Battles of Lexington and Concord. The War was formalized and intensified following the passage of the Lee Resolution, which asserted that the Thirteen Colonies were "Free and independent states", by the Second Continental Congress in Philadelphia on July 2, 1776, and the unanimous ratification of the Declaration of Independence two days later, on July 4, 1776.

Fox Chase also has a Historic Church built in 1888 and branched off to a private school. An Elementary School was also being made underground in 1922, and then WWII came which delayed the process. After the War, it was turned into an above-ground school. There was also a playground a few blocks away. It would be later on when a Philadelphia public school was being built. It was after the WWII and or in the mid-fifties and after the Korean War. Fox Chase and Rockledge saw a building boom of houses in different eras. Farmers were selling off their land.

The father worked for a tree company. He spent most of his time in a place called the Railroad Inn. His mother came over on a boat from England early nineteenth century. People were coming to America because of various reasons. Other countries had problems growing food with seasons. There were other issues, such as Religious Rights and freedom. His mom and dad lived down the street.

His brothers were much younger. He did check on his younger brothers and he also had an older sister. Who was a year older than him? The mother, Blake, rarely saw; she was a hard-working woman, and she worked all the time. She was a hard-working person, coming from Poverty, too. Days and cold nights were going by, and he didn't know anyone from there. Perhaps at this point, he felt lost in and around his older sister.

The summers were hot, and the winters cold. There was no neighbor's next store, in the sense of a block. A bar was across the street and the Railroad station. People were taking the train into

Center City Philadelphia to go to work. There was also a small row of stores, a thrift store and sneakers and or one or two more; occasionally he would walk around to look at things. The neighborhood was built up after the fifties. There really is no more land in and around this area anymore.

Some years went by, and the family moved to Rockledge in late 1964, once again with an older sister and two younger brothers. Rockledge is a borough of Montgomery County Pennsylvania. Abington, Philadelphia, and Cheltenham surround it.

The Borough has a total area of 0.35 square miles. It's also considered a three-mile radius. It has a mayor and a seven-member borough council.

The Borough of Rockledge was formed from Abington Township in the late Nineteenth Century as a result of migration from Philadelphia. Builders bought the farms that were located on what is now Huntingdon Pike and subdivided the tracts into lots for housing. A lot of the mansions stayed. The incorporation of the Borough was on January 9, 1893. By Nineteen hundred, Rockledge had a total population of 500 persons.

Rockledge may have got its name from the old stone quarry which was located on the south side of Huntingdon Pike. The quarry was active between 1916 and 1920. At one point, it reached a depth of over a hundred feet. It was filled in with junk and coal ashes from Philadelphia, Pennsylvania.

In 1888, a gentleman or an owner of a shipping company saw a need for a church close to his summer home. At the time, there may have been 30 summer homes. There were no Churches, and a mission of Trinity was established. Rockledge was a go between two New Hope and N.Y. and Philadelphia.

The elderly gentleman died and his wife wanted to make a memorial to his husband. The original church was on the front of the property and needed to be moved to a higher location. It was uplifted and pulled to its position by mules with greased timber in 1897. The church was built in 1888 out of stone. The dedication of the new building was in 1998.

The Rockledge Volunteer Fire Company was formed in 1903. The fire station is located at 3508 Huntingdon Pike, Rockledge, PA. The fire test came in before WW I when the Knitting mill burned down, briefly threatening the entire Borough. The mill went out of business finally, or perhaps another fire. The vacant building remained for decades to come.

It wasn't long before the owners of the big houses sold off more land and started building more houses.

His place was made of Asbestos shingle and was a twin three-story house with and without finished basements. The suburb's building of homes was not coming to an end; even apartment buildings were being built.

The neighbors knew about one another, and especially on a three block street? The houses were twins, single and a mansion or two in the lower and top part of the street.

When they moved to Rockledge, Blake didn't keep in touch with anyone. When you walked up to the house, you entered an enclosed glass porch that led to the room with a staircase that led upstairs to two bedrooms on the second floor and the third floor, which was divided by a staircase with two rooms with no heat. Unfortunately, the builder didn't supply heating ducts up there. His room was on the right side on the third floor with a single bed with an unfinished closet, which somewhat was a waste of space. His younger brother slept on the other of the room. When you walked in, there was a living room there was another small room, a kitchen, and a bathroom. The house had its problems, one being bad floors walls, drafty, cold in the winter and very hot in the summer. There was no Air-condition T.V. and or a computer. Computers didn't exist at that time. And a T.V. was a luxury. The basement was not dug out deep enough. They had a washer and dryer but you had to duck your head, and the back of the basement was like a dirt hole with a couple pipes running through it.

The original Elementary School was built in 1888 as two rooms. It was later destroyed by fire and rebuilt in 1903. A small school, First grade through sixth grade. He was held back a year. Everyone who grew up there went to that elementary school. There were over a thousand homes.

These were parents with two, three, and four children, and a couple of prominent families with ten children, and there were a couple families with one child. And perhaps there was 45% of two or more parenting and 35% single parenting situation in the Borough? The remaining 20% were elderly couples and elderly singles.

The Borough has everything in and around: a parade every year, a June fate that was in the back of the schoolyard once a year, it had booths to pop balloons and throw darts. There was a water squirt booth to shoot in a clown's mouth and other stands where you could win stuffed animals. There was a cotton candy machine. It was productive entertainment for kids and the community and an excellent way to get to the neighbors.

There was a family-owned hardware store, delicatessen, Danish-Bakery, and hamburger and custard stand. Then, there is a mini Police station and a barber shop. He was an old-style professional Barbra.

Back then he was a person who used warm shaving cream and a straight-edged razor. There were also a few restaurants that had good food and drink and a Nativity Episcopal Church. It also had a few gas stations, a mechanical shop, and a Shriner's club. There was no bank there at this time.

Neighboring Rockledge is Huntingdon Valley and Hollywood and that was a development that was up the street off of Hunting Pike Rd. Some developers came up with an idea to build Hollywood like a Spanish-type architect.

There was a strip mall with a garden center, restaurant, pool hall, bowling alley, car wash, movie theater, and some other stores, what is Hunting Valley shopping center.

At this time, his mother and father were together; his dad would try to fix the floor in the kitchen more than one time. The joists were rotted, and the basement was an unfinished basement and a dirt floor with a low ceiling. Times were taking the clothes from the washer to the dryer to dry. What is a child of 6 years of age to think? I don't know the year the house was built.

There were families across the street. The parents had three boys with a sister. They were four, five, and six years of age that were older. There was a family on the other side of the street with three girls. No one in the family at their age did play with other children, they did their school work, and his mother would make stew and times without cooking and bring home donuts for dinner.

If you didn't eat what was given to you, you went to bed hungry. There were some hungry nights, and it wasn't long, and all of a sudden, the father would be gone. Every day for a while went to school you got to know other kids.

With the parents never around, the kids could go outside. There was somewhat of a backyard with nothing to do with a garage with no roof. There were no bikes or toys at this time. We weren't aware of the Playground. It was a moment in time adjusting to an abusive, dysfunctional situation. Blake believes at this time the mother knew she had made a mistake. Or perhaps the alcohol was more important to their father than his kids and wife. We were raising ourselves. He would go and talk to his sister.

At the bottom of their street was a bakery, and at the other bottom of the hill, there was a small Oil Company with a couple of trucks. There was a building boom of houses being built. For the most part, the homes in Rockledge were gas heat.

Blake Avenue was a street at the beginning. You went up the hill then leveled out, and then went down. And that was eight or so blocks in a row. There is a street that runs in the middle, Montgomery Avenue, from one end to another.

On the other side of the main street are houses too. His mother had registered everyone for school, and it was three and a half blocks away.

We had to walk to a school beginning in first grade. He was held back a year. Everyone who grew up there went to that elementary school. There are over a thousand homes with families who are working and raising their children.

Once you started first grade, you got to know the other children in the neighborhood. On this block, it was a three-block street.

Each family was aware of the others. Generations to follow were being born in the 1950s and 1960s, babies were being formed, and homes were being constructed.

He entered first grade at Rockledge Elementary School and started knowing other children on the block and others in the neighborhood. One family up the hill had four boys, and one was his age with a sister who was a year younger than him. Another family lived down the street and had three boys and two girls. In fact, his neighbor and a joining house had one son. The father worked and was always trying to fix his house. The owner lacked the self-will to do anything. That's when he was introduced to the family across the street. They had four brothers and a sister. Thomas, Joe, Bob, and Billy were a few years older than Blake, and we went and played waffle ball on the lawn, in the back were trees and The Railroad tracks. We put a rope on a tree and would swing over the tracks.

Other people lived on the other side of the Railroad tracks; no one really wanted the train running in their backyard. Later on, people from both sides were constantly building barricades so the train wouldn't get to the train stain. It took a long time, but eventually, that section was closed down. Until this day, I couldn't tell where the train came from.

There was another family across the street that had two sons and kept to themselves. Everyone walked to school every day. Students would sit down in class with teachers who wanted to teach children and took pride in it. They sat down on wooden desks.

Every day, we woke up and walked a block and a half. No one knew what a school bag was; you had to carry your books. Blake followed his sister for years, going to Rockledge Elementary School.

We were going to school and paying attention to the teacher at an early age, you don't know a lot of people. We would come home and do our schoolwork. He started to be a lost child at an early age, feeling lost at five years of age. There was somewhat of a backyard with nothing to do. There were no bikes in the family at this time. They were aware of a Jarred Playground and occasionally went down there. They had a swing set and played board games.

It was a moment in time adjusting to an abusive, dysfunctional father and mother who was rarely seen. Blake believed at this time the mother knew she had made a mistake. Or perhaps the alcohol was more important to their father than his kids and wife?

The father was his birth father and did not do things with you. One thing he didn't do was buy the family shoes or take you somewhere. He would spend as much time as he could in the bars after work. The child has nothing but bad memories about his father. Years went by, and everyone moved up a grade. The school had a gym and a gym night where you could go on Friday nights and play games or Basketball.

The classes were pretty small, perhaps fifteen students in a class, all from the neighborhood. Once a year, you started to know kids your age and their families and then fourth grade came along. At this age, perhaps Blake was wondering what type of life he was headed for.

Rockledge and Philadelphia are also bordered by what is called Lorimar Park. It was a vast place with 200 acres of trees and animals, deer and foxes. You could walk across or down the street and climb the hill to get on the Railroad tracks. The tracks went to the park and beyond. The railroad tracks were a mysterious place. When you walked the Railroad tracks heading to the East, it took you through a canyon. And crossed a road, and you were in the park.

The fascination was a sensation at the end. It ended with this big steel trestle, and all around were trees and some walls of rock, with a stream running below.

They also stayed around the house and played in the yard, and at times, always had a dog. The yard was dirt and hilly there wasn't anything you could do with it. Certainly, there wasn't anything to do inside the house with no T.V. there. Occasionally, we would play waffle ball in the neighbor's front yard across the street.

There was a time when Blake and two brothers from across the street took the tracks to the bridge, where there was a water hole that turned into a small creek that was loaded with fish you could catch by hand.

His mother encouraged the kids to go to Bethany Baptist Church.

It was about three blocks from the house, located in Fox Chase. He went a few times with his sister but felt like an outcast for being poor. He stopped going.

An Independence Day was created on July 4th, 1776 Congress enacted 13 colonies free from King George II. What is known as the 4th of July. It started at one end of Rockledge on Huntingdon pike to the other end.

There were parading people who believed in this great country and their cultures. These were the neighborhood people parading down Huntingdon Pike.

They would wear costumes and party hats with musical bands, floats, bicycles, and mothers pulling their children in red wagons.

Neighbors were coming out from all over and lining both sides of the streets. Café's open to enjoy the bright celebration. The beginning of the summer was here and near. In some respect, at this age, neighbors were somewhat private and picked and chose who to associate with. At times, Once again, for some reason, you don't feel like other people with a dysfunctional family.

In the wintertime, people would get their Red Flyers out and sled down the hill. It was treacherous and dangerous; the turn was so sharp most people couldn't make it and would end up in the trees.

Most of the time, the mother was never around; she was working. Food was scarce occasionally; she would make stew and that meal of food would be for a couple of days. Neighbors didn't help out, and there was no assistance from the Government. There were no food drives, churches and Welfare to help the poor.

Blake was going to Elementary school when he was first introduced to the family up the street and met the whole family including the mother who was becoming sick. They had four brothers and a baby sister.

If there were any structure trying to happen, it wouldn't be long before his whole situation would change. It's assumed they only lived there for three years on Blake Avenue.

It was nine years of age when he knew the family was going to a place called Christ Home in Warminster, Pennsylvania, in 1968. Christ Home was a foster home in 1903. It was a continuous charitable organization founded as a non-denominational Christian Ministry of Life services to both older adults and children with programs and services. Blake's mother told the family their father left, and there wasn't any more talk about him after that.

All of a sudden, his mother sat everyone down and told them they were going into a foster home, and or until she could get on her feet, she said. In 1968 the family was then put into Christ Home. It was sometime in the year before summer when we all arrived. At nine years of age all these things are running through your head. Where are your brothers and sister, nowhere to be seen?

Everyone was dividend up according to age in a separate building. You were somewhat confined to the building. It had a dining hall, church, and a planting field with some older people living in tiny ranch row houses that lived on the property. It was a daily routine of cleaning, school, and denomination. When everyone arrived, they were given a Holy Bible, a Red Letter Edition.

Senior Services was a community where you know one another by neighbors and staff with Independent living, memory care, and nursing. Children's services provide residential programs, transit living for teens, and baby programs. However, things were different in 1968.

If Blake got a chance to read all types of articles he would. With your family on your mind you think about your brothers and sister who you never saw on the property. Blake was put in some building.

He was somewhat confused and rebellious. Couldn't go anywhere shopping or to a park, and or whatsoever, imprisoned. Blake spent his 4th-grade childhood there.

Perhaps Blake cannot recall what happened when he was introduced to the Paddle. The Paddle was a row boat oar that was cut down to size with holes driven in it for spanking. At some point in time, under the circumstances, you have to survive on their terms. He always felt hungry, even as a younger child. You were always hungry with small portions of food. It was in the summer when they told me he had to go out to the fields and pick crops and food. They sent the kids outside to work in the fields all day for days in the hot sun. They were poor people who were isolated and felt Unwanted in the community, labeled unjustly as bad kids. There were kids there from all over and even out of State. It wasn't long before school started.

They introduced him to an elderly gentleman whom they sent him to see, and he talked about Godly issues with The Holy Bible. The King James Version: Red-letter. A place to work us and not allowed to see your family at times feeling lost. There wasn't any good memory, and it started before I even went there at an earlier age. Their program, in a way, was meaningful. He couldn't connect or he felt like he could not connect to God.

The kids were poor people whose parents couldn't afford to take care of them at the time. A single parent with no help and no education, you had to do manual labor work. In this case, his mother was a waitress working for cents an hour, plus tips, and it could have been less.

Only times were not the greatest. There was very little talk about it at the time. He never saw his brothers and sister there we were all divided up in other buildings.

And they had schools with the State standards for learning. They taught the introductory courses in Elementary teaching. There was a small class of people. He cannot recall much about it. The room they gave you was an old metal bed with a 6-inch mattress. In their eyes, they saw it as a path to Christianity. It all felt like an uncertainty of direction in life. What do you think at nine years of age and your mother put you away in a home? Blake could have been traumatized because of what happened just before he arrived.

There was a rumor all over the newspaper and radio and talked about that a senator was killed. Robert Kennedy (November 20, 1925 – June 6, 1968), also known by his initials RFK and by the nickname Bobby, was an American politician and lawyer.

He served as the 64th United States attorney general from January 1961 to September 1964 and as a U.S. senator from New York from January 1965 until his assassination in June 1968, when he was running for the Democratic presidential nomination. Like his brothers, John F. Kennedy and Ted Kennedy, he was a prominent member of the Democratic Party and is viewed by some historians as an icon of modern liberalism.

Kennedy was born into a wealthy political family in Brookline, Massachusetts. After serving in the U.S. Naval Reserve from 1944 to 1946, Kennedy returned to his studies at Harvard University and later received his law degree from the University of Virginia. He began his career as a correspondent for The Boston Post and as a lawyer at the Justice Department, but later resigned to manage his brother John's successful campaign for the U.S. Senate in 1952.

The following year, he worked as an assistant counsel to the Senate committee chaired by Senator Joseph McCarthy. He gained national attention as the chief counsel of the Senate Labor Rackets Committee from 1957 to 1959, where he publicly challenged Teamsters President Jimmy Hoffa over the union's practices. Kennedy resigned from the committee to conduct his brother's successful campaign in the 1960 presidential election. He was appointed United States attorney general at the age of 35, one of the youngest cabinet members in American history. He served as his brother's closest advisor until the latter's assassination in 1963.

His political ploy during his tenure was known for advocating for the civil rights movement and the fight against organized crime even though his family had a history with them. He was no Saint when he was said to be a womanizer. He toyed with U.S. foreign policy related to Cuba. He authored his account of the Cuban Missile Crisis in a book titled Thirteen Days. As attorney general, he authorized the

Federal Bureau of Investigation (FBI) to wiretap Martin Luther King Jr. After his brother's assassination, he remained in office during the Presidency of Lyndon B. Johnson for several months. He left to run for the United States Senate from New York in 1964 and defeated Republican incumbent Kenneth Keating, overcoming criticism that he was a "carpetbagger" from Massachusetts. In office, Kennedy was for U.S. involvement in the Vietnam War and did not raise awareness of Poverty by sponsoring legislation designed to lure private business.

He pretended to be an advocate for issues related to human rights and social justice that, in the long run, couldn't be fixed by traveling abroad to Eastern Europe, Latin America, and South Africa and forming working relationships with Martin Luther King Jr. Cesar Chavez.

In 1968, Robert became a leading candidate for the Democratic nomination for the Presidency by appealing to poor African Americans, Hispanics, Catholics, and young voters.

Shortly after winning the California primary around midnight on June 5, 1968, Kennedy was shot by Sirhan, a 24-year-old Palestinian, allegedly in retaliation for his support of Israel following the 1967 Six-Day War. Kennedy died 25 hours later. Sirhan was arrested, tried, and convicted, though Kennedy's assassination, like his brother, continues to be the subject of widespread analysis and numerous conspiracy theories.

Suppose Blake got a chance he would read all types of articles. With your family on your mind you think about your brothers and sister who you never saw on the property. Blake was put in some building.

Perhaps Blake cannot recall what happened when he was introduced to the Paddle. The Paddle was a row boat oar that was cut down to size with holes driven in it for spanking. At some point in time, under the circumstances, you have to survive on their terms. He always felt hungry, even as a younger child. You were always hungry with small portions of food. It was in the summer when they told me he had to go out to the fields and pick crops and food. They sent the kids outside to work in the fields all day for days in 100-degree weather. They were poor people who were isolated and felt Unwanted in the community, labeled unjustly as bad kids. There were kids there from all over and even out of State. It wasn't long before school started. They gave everyone a copy of The Holy Bible. The King James Version: Red-letter. A place to work and not allowed to see your family at times feeling lost. There wasn't any good memory, and it started before he even went there at an earlier age. Their program, in a way, was not meaningful. He couldn't connect or he felt like he could not connect to God.

The kids were poor people whose parents couldn't afford to take care of them at the time. A single parent with no help and no education, you had to do manual labor work. In this case, his mother was a waitress working for cents an hour, plus tips, and it could have been less.

Only times were not the greatest. There was very little talk about it at the time. He never saw his brothers and sister they were all divided up in other buildings.

And they had schools with the State standards for learning. They taught the basic courses in Elementary teaching. There was a small class of people. He cannot recall much about it. In your room, they gave you an old metal bed with a 6-inch mattress. In their eyes, they saw it as a path to Christianity. It all felt like an uncertainty of direction in life. What do you think at nine years of age and your mother put you away in a home? Blake could have been traumatized because of what happened just before he arrived.

A year went by, and before they knew it, their mother came back for us. The family moved back to Rockledge. As soon as the mother took over the house, she had a chimney built in the middle room. The mother hired an Italian Masonry man, and so she could install a Pot Belly, wood stove. That was the heat gathering wood wherever you could and burning it.

The house came with gas heat. Until this day, he wondered why it was kept off, and on the other hand, it could have been about something vague: turn your gas off to save money or down to a minimal function. We had a gas stove. When they build houses, the thermostat is usually in the first room. In the winter, when you open your front door and shut it and or draft triggers the thermostat and turns the heater on. The father was out of the picture.

The mother worked all the time as a waitress and slept on the couch. The oldest daughter slept upstairs in one of two bedrooms on the second floor. The older of the two males lived on the third floor, separated by a stairway. The walls were made out of broken old plasterboard, horsehair? Behind the plaster were strips of wood. A vast hole hovered over his bed.

He went back to Elementary school for 5th through 6th grade. The family was all back together, or should I say and or what he would say; there was no more talk about the father gone.

The way the house was built and because the sun rose on the East, the summers were hot, and the winters were cold because there were no heating ducts on the third floor. And as usual, time was going by.

The school was going, but all the other children were enrolled. The mother was working, and the older sister took on responsibilities.

He started getting friendly with the family up the street. The father escaped WWII and came to America. He started out working as a skilled Mason—any type of Brick, Stone, Stucco, Block, Concrete, and Fireplace.

He studied Masonry in Italy. It was not long before he started his own company. They had a ping pong table, Dartboard, wooden Bar, and a wood stove in the basement. The father made Masons in the neighborhood. The dad was another one who wouldn't turn his gas on. He built a den and put a wood stove, and on the second floor he put a small coal stove at the top of the stairs. He would pick up wood from the job and have it split.

. They called him Pop and he built an addition on the back with a fireplace, and then he hooked up a wood stove to the fireplace. And a coal stove on the second floor. His dad had a log splitter, and they would pick up wood here and there for free and heat the house. He was another one who would not run gas heat for heat.

You had to labor for a while, and then you were taught bricklaying, block laying, piers, footers, walls, and chimneys, fireplaces. His two brothers eventually became masons.

The ‘60s were here, and also saw the longest steel and airline strike in American history but also agreed on a wage increase. J.F.K. signs the Fair Labor Act, increasing the minimum wage from 1 dollar to 1.25 by September. The Tax Foundation reported that 25 percent of American workers’ earnings are taxed.

Title VII of the Civil Rights Act of 1964 made job discrimination illegal. Yet the Federal Government agency created to enforce this law, the Equal Opportunity Commission, failed to act on behalf of women for most of the Sixties, instead focusing on minorities, under pressure from women activists at the beginning. The EEOC finally began to help women workers by filing gender discrimination lawsuits against companies. Occupational barriers began to fall.

The ‘60s was also seeing The Vietnam War. The Vietnam War (also known by other names) was a conflict in Vietnam, Laos, and Cambodia from 1 November 1955 to the fall of Saigon on 30 April 1975. It was the second of the Indochina Wars and was a significant conflict of the Cold War. While the War was officially fought between North Vietnam and South Vietnam, the North was supported by the Soviet Union, China, and other communist states. In contrast, the South was supported by the United States and other anti-communist allies, making the War a proxy war between the United States and the Soviet Union. It lasted almost 20 years, with direct U.S. military involvement. The conflict also spilled over into neighboring states, exacerbating the Laotian Civil War and the Cambodian Civil War, which ended with all three countries officially becoming communist states.

After the fall of French Indochina with the 1954 Geneva Conference on 21 July, the country gained independence from France. Still, it was divided into two parts: The Viet Minh took control of North Vietnam, while the U.S. assumed financial and military support for South Vietnam. The Viet Cong (VC), a South Vietnamese common front under the direction of the North, initiated a guerrilla war in the South. The People's Army of Vietnam (PAVN), also known as the North Vietnamese Army (NVA), engaged in more conventional warfare with the U.S. Army of the Republic of Vietnam (ARVN) forces. North Vietnam invaded Laos in 1958, establishing the Ho Chi Minh Trail to supply and reinforce the VC. By 1963, the North had sent 40,000 soldiers to fight in the South. U.S. involvement increased under President John F. Kennedy, from just under a thousand military advisors in 1959 to 23,000 by 1964. Furthermore, when Johnson was president, he sent an additional 150,000 Americans.

Lyndon B. Johnson took the Presidency in 1964 after J.F.K. was assassinated during the Cold War. Prior to his Presidency, the U.S. was already involved in the Vietnam War. He also knew we couldn't win and passed the Gulf Tonkin Resolution, which granted Johnson the power to launch a full-scale military operation in Southeast Asia. The number of military personnel increased, and casualties soared among U.S. soldiers.

The communist Offensive flamed the antiwar movement, especially among the draft age and students on campuses, and public opinion turned against American involvement. Johnson's administration continued to promote political cooperation and integration as his predecessors had.

The sociology theory of a generation gap first came to light in the 1960s, when the younger generation (later known as baby boomers) seemed to go against everything their parents had believed in terms of music, values, and governmental and political views. People were protesting the War at colleges. There was a saying among this generation (Peace, Pot, and Microdot.)

Communist Party USA, officially the Communist Party of the United States of America (CPUSA), also known as the American Communist Party, is a Marxist–Leninist and Dictatorship communist party in the United States which was established in 1919 after a split in the Socialist Party of America following the Russian Revolution.

The history of the CPUSA is closely related to the history of the American labor movement and the history of communist parties worldwide. Initially operating underground due to the Palmer Raids, which started during the First Red Scare, the party was influential in American politics in the first half of the 20th century, and it also played a prominent role in the history of the labor movement. Its membership increased during the Great Depression, and it also played a key role in the founding of the Congress of Industrial Organizations, which did no good.

The CPUSA subsequently declined due to events such as World War II, the beginning of the second Red Scare, and the influence of McCarthyism. Its opposition to the Marshall Plan and the Truman Doctrine was unpopular, with its endorsed candidate, Henry A. Wallace, underperforming in the 1948 presidential election. Its support for the Soviet Union increasingly alienated it from the rest of the left in the United States in the 1960s.

The CPUSA received significant funding from the Soviet Union and crafted its public positions to match those of Moscow. The CPUSA also used a covert apparatus to assist the Soviets with their intelligence activities in the United States and utilized a network of front organizations to shape public opinion.

During the first half of the 20th century, the Communist Party was influential in various struggles for democratic rights. It played a prominent role in the labor movement from the 1920s through the 1940s, having a major hand in founding most of the country's first industrial unions. (which would later use the McCarran Internal Security Act to expel their communist members). But they are here.

A Historian concluded that decades of recent scholarship offer "a more nuanced portrayal of the party as both a Stalinist sect tied to a vicious regime and the most dynamic organization within the American Left during the 1930s and '40s." Communism was the first political party in the United States.

Two men dressed in suits are surrounded by persons holding signs. Defendants Bob Thompson and Ben Davis were supporters in 1949-1958.

One hundred forty-four leaders of the Communist Party in the U.S.A. violated the Smith Act by conspiring to overthrow the Government. The Federal courthouses in New York, Los Angeles, Honolulu, Pittsburgh, Philadelphia, Cleveland, Seattle, Baltimore, Seattle, Detroit, St. Louis, Denver, Boston, Puerto Rico, and New Haven. The outcome of over 100 convictions, with sentences up to six years in prison and each a $10,000 fine

The Smith Act trials of Communist Party leaders in New York City from 1949 to 1958 were the result of US federal government prosecutions in the postwar period and during the Cold War between the Soviet Union and the United States. Leaders of the Communist Party of the United States (CPUSA) were accused of violating the Smith Act, a statute that prohibited advocating violent overthrow of the Government. The defendants argued that they advocated a transition to socialism and that the First Amendment's guarantee of freedom of speech and association protected their membership in a political party. Appeals from these trials reached the US Supreme Court, which ruled on issues in Dennis v. United States (1951) and Yates v. United States (1957).

The first trial of eleven communist leaders was held in New York in 1949; it was one of the lengthiest trials in United States history. Numerous supporters of the defendants protested outside the courthouse on a daily basis. The trial was featured twice on the cover of Time magazine. The defense frequently antagonized the judge and prosecution; five defendants were jailed for contempt of court because they disrupted the proceedings.

The prosecution's case relied on undercover informants, who described the goals of the CPUSA, interpreted communist texts, and testified of their knowledge that the CPUSA advocated the violent overthrow of the US government.

While the first trial was underway, events outside the courtroom influenced public perception of communism: The Soviet Union tested its first nuclear weapon, and communists prevailed in the Chinese Civil War. In this period, the House Un-American Activities

Committee (HUAC) had also begun conducting investigations and hearings of writers and producers in Hollywood suspected of communist influence.

Public opinion was overwhelmingly against the defendants in New York. After a 10-month trial, the jury found all 11 defendants guilty. The judge sentenced them to terms of up to five years in federal prison, and sentenced all five defense attorneys to imprisonment for contempt of court. Two of the attorneys were subsequently disbarred.

After the first trial, the prosecutors – encouraged by their success – prosecuted more than 100 additional CPUSA officers for violating the Smith Act. Some were tried solely because they were members of the party. Many of these defendants had difficulty finding attorneys to represent them. The trials decimated the leadership of the CPUSA. In 1957, eight years after the first trial, the US Supreme Court's Yates decision brought an end to similar prosecutions. It ruled that defendants could be prosecuted only for their actions, not for their beliefs.

The CPUSA received significant funding from the Soviet Union and crafted its public positions to match those of Moscow. The CPUSA also used a covert apparatus to assist the Soviets with their intelligence activities in the United States and utilized a network of front organizations to shape public opinion. CPUSA opposed glasnost and perestroika in the Soviet Union, and as a result, significant funding from the Communist Party of the Soviet Union never ended.

The Woodstock Music Fair was the most famous of the 1960s rock festival, held on a farm property in New York in August for three days. It was organized by four inexperienced promoters, who nonetheless signed a who's who of current rock acts, including Jimi Hendrix, Sly and the Family Stone, the Who, Grateful Dead, Janice Joplin, the Jefferson Airplane, and others.

The festival began to go wrong almost immediately when the towns of both Woodstock and Wallkill, New York, denied permission to stage it.

Nevertheless, they signed a who's who of current rock acts, including Jimi Hendrix, Sly and the Family Stone, the Who, Grateful Dead, Janice Joplin, the Jefferson Airplane, and others.

Furthermore, the name Woodstock was retained because of the cachet of hipness associated with the town, where Bob Dylan and other musicians were living. The farmer made his land available for the festival.

A few tickets were sold, but some 400,000 people showed up demanding free entry, which they got. Rain then turned the place into a sea of mud, but somehow the audience bonded. Large amounts of psychedelics (Blotter Acid) were consumed. The 1960s term also refers to an era more often called the Sixties and also musical Geniuses, and these were just some of them.

Jefferson Airplane was part of a counterculture movement of the 1960s and helped pioneer psychedelic rock. They were the first rock act from California to achieve success. Their songs from "Surrealistic Pillow" became the soundtrack of Summer Love. They got so popular they made music in the U.K.

Mamas and the Papas were also becoming above some, because of their immaculate harmonies that was good. These folk rockers had a sense of hits that made them icons. They also had a fair share of controversies, drama, and tensions. The fact is their songs remain well-named classics.

The Beach Boys became popular; some of it was a California sound. They were musical masterpieces. Pet Sounds made them rock legends. They pushed their records when it came to making music. In fact, it was Pet Sounds that inspired Paul McCarthy and the rest of the Beatles to make Sgt—Pepper's Lonely Hearts Club Band.

The Beatles were an English rock band formed in Liverpool in 1960. There was Paul McCartney, John Lennon, George Harrison, and Ringo Star. They are some of the most influential bands of all time and were integral to the development of the 1960s counterculture and widespread music recognition as an Art form.

Their sound incorporated elements of classical music and traditional pop in innovative ways; the band also explored music styles from folk, psychedelic, and hard rock.

The Beatles revolutionized many aspects of the music and were published by their followers.

The Monkees were formed in 1965 for the situation of comedy sense. The input was limited for the first few years and even after the show was canceled. They had lineup changes over the years, but it was in the 60s when they truly made a name for themselves.

Vocalist and drummer Mickey Dolenz once described. The Monkees, as a TV show about an imaginary band that wanted to be the Beetles but was never successful, but they bounced back. They have sold 75 million records worldwide.

Frank Zappa was known for his works and his contribution to rock, which cannot be stated enough. He was fearless in his experimentations and improvisations. He did not subscribe to what is conventional at times. He liked to break rules-musically, at least. He made stellar music and was controversial at times, but that didn't stop him.

The Doors were immortalized with a string of hits that catapulted them to fame. Jim Morrison, for all his performances and unpredictability, on and off stage, was a talented musician and poet. At times, he captivated the audience, and his spoken words could be haunting.

The Byrds made enough impact to make a name for themselves with their sounds and style that is also still heard. They introduced folk rock to the masses and helped in the country rocks thanks to the addition of Gram Parsons. Even though their career will be short-lived compared to their peers, their members went on to achieve success by joining other groups and pursuing solo.

There were also sets of political and cultural trends. The Social revolution was part of a broader counterculture. The 1960s was a diverse decade in American history. The Black Panther Party was formed by two guys from Chicago that spread throughout the country. It was an Anti-Law Enforcement Party.

Martin Luther King. (born Michael King January 15, 1939 – April 4, 1968) was an American Baptist minister and activist who was one of the leaders in the civil rights movement from 1955 until his assassination in 1968 coming out of a motel. There were rumors he was a womanizer and or the woman in the hotel was not his wife.

A Black church leader and a son of early civil rights activist and minister Martin Luther King Sr., King advanced civil rights for people of color in the United States through nonviolence and civil disobedience. Inspired by his own beliefs and the nonviolent activism of Mahatma Gandhi, he led targeted, nonviolent resistance against Jim Crow laws and other forms of discrimination in the United States.

King participated in and led marches for the right to vote, desegregation, labor rights, and other civil rights. He oversaw the 1955 Montgomery bus boycott and later became the first president of the Southern Christian Leadership Conference (SCLC). As president of the SCLC, he led the unsuccessful Albany Movement in Albany, Georgia, and helped organize some of the nonviolent 1963 protests in Birmingham, Alabama. King was one of the leaders of the 1963 March on Washington, where he delivered his "I Have a Dream" speech on the steps of the Lincoln Memorial. The civil rights movement achieved pivotal legislative gains in the Civil Rights Act of 1964, the Voting Rights Act of 1965, and the Fair Housing Act for black minorities in 1968.

The SCLC put into practice the tactics of nonviolent protest with success by strategically choosing the methods and places in which protests were carried out. There were several dramatic standoffs with segregationist authorities, who frequently responded non-violently. King was jailed several times.

The Federal Bureau of Investigation (FBI) director J. Edgar

Hoover considered King a radical and made him an object of the FBI's COINTELPRO from 1963 forward. FBI agents investigated him for communist ties.

He also helped some of the nonviolent protests in Birmingham, Alabama. He also led the protest, where he delivered his “I Have a Dream” speech in Washington. The SCLC put into practice the tactics of nonviolent protest with success, knowing that it had to be done by them peacefully by strategy, choosing the methods and places in which protests were carried out. Dr. King took sides with NOI and Louis Farrakhan. You will draw your conclusion if you follow up about them.

# The Seventies

The seventies were here, and The War on Drugs began in June 1971 when Richard Nixon declared it to be "Public Enemy Number One" and increased Federal funding for drug control agencies and treatment programs.

South Florida was a postcard corner of the Sunshine State, that lush strip of hibiscus and condominiums stretching roughly from Palm Beach south to Key West—is a region in trouble. An epidemic of violent crime, a plague of illicit drugs, and a tidal wave of refugees have slammed into South Florida with the destructive power of a hurricane. Those three forces, and a number of lesser ills, threaten to turn one of the nation's most prosperous, congenial, and naturally gorgeous regions into a paradise lost.

When the FBI issued its annual list of the ten most crime-ridden cities in the nation last September, three of them were in South Florida: Miami (pop. 347,000) was in first place, West Palm Beach (pop. 63,000) was fifth, and Fort Lauderdale (pop. 153,000) was eighth. Miami last year had the nation's highest murder rate, 70 per 100,000 residents, and this year's pace has been even higher.

An estimated 70% of all cocaine imported into the U.S. passes through South Florida. Drug smuggling could be the region's major industry, worth anywhere from $7 billion to $12 billion a year (vs. $12 billion for real estate and $9 billion for tourism, the area's two biggest legitimate businesses). Miami's Federal Reserve branch has a currency surplus of $5 billion, mostly in drug-generated $50 and $100 bills, or more than the nation's twelve Federal Reserve banks combined. Drug money has corrupted banking, real estate, law enforcement, and even the fishing industry, whose practitioners are abandoning the pursuit of snapper and grouper for the transport of bales of marijuana (square grouper) as fishermen call it) from freighters at sea to the mainland. About one-third of the region's murders are drug-related. In addition, 25,000 refugees have arrived from Haiti; boatloads of half-starved Haitians are washing up on the area's beaches every week. The wave of illegal immigrants has pushed up unemployment, taxed social services, irritated racial tensions, and helped send the crime rate to staggering heights. Marielitos are believed to be responsible for half of all violent crimes in Miami.

The Latins are gradually turning the region into their own colony. Of the 1.7 million residents of Dade County (Miami and environs), 39% are Hispanic (vs. 34% white and 27% black). It is estimated that the Latins will become a majority in Dade, outnumbering non-Latin whites 43% to 42%.

The bloodiest crimes tend to be committed by drug dealers and refugees, and often that warfare is intramural. One man was shot as he walked from his apartment building in Miami; injured, he was taken to Miami's Mercy Hospital, where he was again shot, this time fatally, in his bed. As Eric Gonzalez and his twelve-year-old son Eric were getting out of their car in front of their home in North Miami, another car raced by spraying machine-gun fire; both father and son were killed. (Twenty--three percent of Miami's murders last year were committed with machine guns, a favorite weapon of drug dealers.) So many bodies now fill the Miami morgue that Dade County Medical Examiner Joe Davis has rented a refrigerated hamburger van to house the overflow. "If you stay here, you have to arm yourself to the teeth, put bars on the windows, and stay at home at all times". I've been through one war and the combat zone, and that is as dangerous as Dade County.

South Florida is just beginning to be the crime capital of the nation, but it has been the drug capital for a decade. Smuggling dope into the region is about as difficult as buying a souvenir in Miami Beach.

"They land it in everything but a bathtub' marvels Patrolman Doug Morris of the Dade County public safety marine patrol, whose dozen men and six boats help patrol the 550 sq. mi. of county waterways." Hell, they even fly coke in from a ship in one of those remote-controlled toy planes and land it on a bay shore condo.

A favorite strategy of cocaine smugglers is for a drug-laden "mother ship" usually an aging freighter, to sail from Colombia or the Caribbean and then stay bobbing 50 miles or so off the Florida coast. On long hauls, drug runners motor out to the mother ship in yachts and fishing boats to pick up the cargo and then shuttle back to the mainland, docking anywhere along some 3,000 miles of South Florida coastline; on shorter hauls, they roar out in souped-up racing speedboats, called "cigarette boats" after the tobacco-bootlegging vessels of the 1930s. Costing as much as $250,000 and able to reach speeds of up to 70 m.p.h., many of the cigarette boats are outfitted with such sophisticated equipment as radar scanners and infra-red night-vision scopes. Cocaine, however, is usually flown into the U.S. by airplane. Customs officials estimate that some 80 planes secretly land in the U.S. every night carrying cargos of white powder, most of them landing in South Florida.

Battling the dope runners are the combined forces of the U.S. Customs Service, the Coast Guard, and the Drug Enforcement Administration, as well as local lawmen. But they all are fighting a losing battle. Last year, law enforcement officials seized 3.2 million lbs. of marijuana, with a street value of $ 1.3 billion, and 2,353 lbs. of cocaine worth $5.8 billion, in and around South Florida. So much dope was seized that the police began trucking it to the Florida Power and Light Co. to burn in its generators (732 lbs. of marijuana equal 1 bbl. of oil, one of the odder statistics to emerge from the region). Yet officials estimate that perhaps as much as ten times the amount seized was smuggled into the region. At the moment, Bade County police have a stash of 162,000 lbs. of marijuana waiting to be entered as evidence in court cases. The Customs Service has 200 seized cigarette boats and 50 airplanes, including a World War II-era A26 bomber that was, ironically, used by Customs agents on drug cases before it was bought by a drug ring.

Anglos tend to work the marijuana trade, while the cocaine market is controlled by Colombians and Cubans in this region. No matter what their specialty, the illegal entrepreneurs can be easily spotted. Young Anglos wearing scruffy Levi's and T-shirts, gold Rolex watches, and ropes of gold chain sit around the marinas waiting for the next call from a mother ship. Current pay for one night's work piloting a "cigarette" averages $50,000, while the wages for unloading the bales are $5,000 to $10,000 a night.

Cuban dealers favor Mercedes Benzes and bodyguards dressed in dark suits and carrying two guns (one under the coat and one strapped to the ankle). José Cruz, nicknamed El Pedrina, always travels in a

Rolls-Royce protected by cars full of bodyguards. Cruz, who is fond of listening to the theme song from The Godfather on his car stereo, never talks on the telephone and keeps himself insulated from any drug deal through relatives and friends. Nevertheless, he was recently convicted for tax evasion.

The billions in narcotics bucks, as police have dubbed the drug money, allow its recipients to buy, in cash, $1 million waterfront homes, $50,000 Mercedes, and $400 bottles of wine. One drug kingpin alone has bought up some $20 million worth of prime Miami real estate. Says Miami Financial Analyst Charles Kimball: “Criminals have become conspicuous buyers of some of the best properties in South Florida”.

Most, if not all, of Miami's 250 banks have drug money in their accounts. As many as 40 banks still neglect to report cash deposits of $10,000 or more, as required by law. And at least four banks, according to law enforcement officials, are controlled by drug dealers. Treasury Department investigators have long suspected that some smaller banks, known as Coin-o-Washes among both cops and criminals, were founded primarily to launder money for the drug trade (see box).

Perhaps the most valuable commodity bought by all that cash is freedom. Once caught, suspected drug dealers are often released on bail of $1 million or more. They typically pay it within hours, sometimes in cash, and skip town. Dealers regard the forfeited bail as merely a cost of doing business. If a prosecutor's case is airtight, money can sometimes pry it open. “We pay for what we need as we need it” one lawyer bragged. “If we can't bribe the cop, we try to bribe the prosecutor, and if we can't get the prosecutor, we try to buy the judge”.

Blake was also friends with another family’s son, who was the same age and lived down the street. We were going down to the basement playing ping pong and darts and having some beer. At this time, we were going to a 7th and 8th grade school being bused to Huntingdon Junior High.

Blake and the boy down the street were hanging around some time at the end of eighth grade and were cutting school, drinking beer, and riding around in a 52 Chevy or a 54. His father owned a gas station with a Mechanic shop three blocks away in Fox Chase.

It all seems fun at the time when you’re failing on the report card, only Blake did pass 8th grade.

Once you got to ninth grade, you were introduced to other people in Abington Township. He felt like a lost soul who had no idea about a purpose in life.

The tracks led to a park that went through a rock canyon, and beyond that was a peaceful, picturesque place. There weren’t enough commuters, so they closed down that section. Fox Chase station is one that goes into Center City.

There were times we had to split firewood. He was another person who didn’t believe in using gas to heat his house, only for cooking, and It may have been an electric stove. He had a wood pot belly stove in the basement, coal stove on the second floor, and a wood stove in the den. There were other people who felt the same way even until this day. However, in today’s world, perhaps there is a slight decline.

For some of us, Gas and Oil heat was expensive, and perhaps the elderly in the fifties and sixties saw something no one else did.

At this time drinking beer and cutting school was a problem. Sometimes, going behind the Bowling alleys and meeting up with other neighboring kids. There are small developments next to Rockledge called Hollywood and Huntingdon Valley, Cheltenham, and Philadelphia. All were neighbors of Rockledge.

Blake knew people from Hollywood and Huntingdon Valley who would meet up at the top of the parking lot, old heads. At fifteen, we were getting served in the Hollywood Tavern and the Deli; you had to get someone of age. The beer distributor was in the back with cases of beer for 5.00 dollars if you knew someone. Sooner or later, everything catches up with you; we all failed ninth grade. Of course, cars were out and there were a few people when they turned 16 they got a license. It was this summer when Blake and his friends would go down the Jeans Hospital fair. A bunch of us would have a few beers and walk down in the night time. It would last for a weekend. They had become friends with some people from Hollywood. The Fair had rides and games.

Blake started going up to The Huntingdon Valley shopping center. There were a bunch of older guys that rode motorcycles. The top of the shopping center lot, an older crowd hung up there. The shopping center had a movie theater where we would go for free. Delicatessen, restaurant that really we could not afford. We could get into the pool hall. Beyond that, it was Lower Moreland, some more rich people. The old heads would get us beer and we would go behind the Bowling Alleys and drink.

There was talk of marijuana in the neighborhood and rumors of The President of Panama, Noriega was bringing in boatloads to America. It was called Panama Red. There were others such as Acapulco gold and some lower grade. Cocaine was around, but it was for the rich they said in Huntingdon Valley.

Blake knew his brother, who had the connections. It seemed or looked like marijuana was becoming popular. He was already drinking alcohol or beer. One of the neighbors always had a case of beer around in the garage. At that time, he was friends with the youngest son who he started to drink with. The family up the street had a pool table in the living room. A Ping Pong table radio and a dart board in the basement.

President Nixon ended the Vietnam War and was withdrawing troops out in 1971, even up until 1976. There was talk about a Journalist who was sent to Vietnam that did some witting reporting to Washington we couldn't win the War, and that is referred as The Pentagon Papers.

The Pentagon Papers also revealed that in the early seventies, Lyndon B Johnson and J.F.K had continued to send American troops over knowingly the War could not be won.

People saw the conflict fought by an expanded ARVN, with U.S. forces being sidelined and increasingly demoralized by domestic opposition which reduced recruitment. It was said N.A.T.O. was Policing the war, and perhaps there was doubt we could have won.

North Vietnam was supported by the Soviet Union and China. South Vietnam was supported by the United States. Some people considered this a Cold War- proxy era.

It lasted almost 18 years with direct U.S. involvement and included The Laotian Civil War and The Cambodian War, which ended in all three Communist states.

A Nation that forgets its past has no future. Understanding that learning about your history is not about making any one person or people feel guilty.

You cannot be guilty that took place before you were born. (Winston Churchill)

Richard Nixon became the next president and was the only President in history to put a freeze on food prices. He was pulling the country out of Inflation. Furthermore, what started the bugging process was Nixon found out the D.N.C. had bugged a meeting of Republicans.

The Watergate scandal was a major political scandal in the United States involving the administration of President Richard Nixon from 1971 to 1974 that led to Nixon's resignation. The scandal stemmed from the Nixon administration. There were continued attempts to cover up its involvement in June. 1972. Break-in of the Democratic National Committee headquarters at Washington D.C. Watergate office building.

After the five perpetrators were arrested, the Press and the Justice Department connected the cash found on them at the time to the Committee for the Re-Election of the President. Further investigations, along with revelations during subsequent trials for burglars, led the House of Representatives to grant the U.S.

House Judiciary Committee additional investigation authority- to probe into "certain matters within its jurisdiction" and that led the Senate to create the U.S. Senate Watergate Committee, which led hearings. Witnesses testified that Nixon had approved plans to cover up his administration's involvement in the brake in and that was a voice-activated taping system in the Oval Office.

Throughout the investigation, Nixon's administration resisted its probes, which led to a constitutional crisis. The Senate Watergate hearings were broadcast "gavel-to-gavel" nationwide by PBS, and this aroused public interest.

Several major revelations and egregious presidential actions obstructing the investigation later in 1973 prompted the House to commence an impeachment process against Nixon. The U.S. Supreme Court ruled that Nixon had to release the Oval Office tapes to government investigators.

The Nixon White House tapes revealed that he had conspired to cover up activities that took place after the break-in and had later tried to use Federal officials to deflect attention from the investigation.

The House Judiciary approved three articles of impeachment against Nixon for obstruction of justice, abuse of power, and contempt of Congress.

With his complicity in the cover-up made public, and his political support completely eroded. Nixon resigned from office on August 8, 1974. It is generally believed that if he had not done so, he would have been impeached by the House and removed from office by a trial in the Senate. He is the only U.S. president to have resigned from office.

On September 8, 1974, his successor, Gerald Ford, pardoned Nixon.

There were 69 people indicted and 48 people- many of them top Nixon administration officials-convicted. The metonym Watergate came to encompass an array of clandestine and often illegal activities undertaken by members of the Nixon administration, including bugging the offices of political opponents and people of whom Nixon or his officials were suspicious, ordering investigations of activist groups and political figures and using The Federal Bureau of Investigations' and, the Central Intelligence Agency, and internal Revenue as political weapons. The use of the suffix-gate after an identifying term has since become synonymous with public scandal, especially political scandal.

After President Nixon's resignation, Gerald Ford became President he Pardoned Nixon and shifted to being an advocate for the White House agenda. Congress passed several of Nixon's proposals, including the National Environmental Policy Act. It was a commendable thing to do. Another high-profile victory for the Republicans was the State and Local Fiscal Assistance Act passed in 1972.

The act established a Revenue Sharing program for state and local governments. Ford's leadership was instrumental in shepherding revenue sharing.

Many remember the 1970s as a decade of a soaring economy, political upheaval, and the revision of the United States.

But the significance of the seventies goes beyond high gas prices. The Watergate and Vietnam made a profound change to American politics, social norms, and the nation's economy.

In 1971, for the first time, the census counted over 200 million people living in the United States. The 13.4% increase since the last census indicated that 203, 302, 031 populations now called the U.S.A. home.

It had taken only fifty years to go from the first hundred million censuses in 1920 to the second. Once again, the geographic center of the United States was in Illinois.

The 1970s were famous for bell bottoms, an economic struggle, and culture change, technological innovation, and disco.

There was another rise in the building Industry, and at one time, they had some of the biggest Lobbyists in Washington. It was also said that less than a decade ago, journalists were saying America is become overpopulated and that causes your Taxes to increase.

There were subgenres of rock music, and hard rock, and heavy metal achieved considerable success. Other genres, such as reggae, were innovated throughout the decade and grew in popularity Hip Hop also emerged but did not become popular until the following decade. Classical music lost its momentum. However, through the invention and theoretical development, this particular gave rise to experimental classical and minimalist music by classical composers. Alongside the popularity of experimental with the continued development of synthesizers, more composers embraced this particular genre, gaining the notice of listeners who were looking for something new and different. Therefore, rock bands and single artists and were already popping up in the seventies.

During a time when women's liberation made headlines, ladies of legends of country music made a meaningful impact in the genre, telling their stories through their songs. Some of the most iconic music queens recorded hit records.

Here are some, Dolly Parton, Ann Murry, Linda Ronstadt, Judd, and Olivia Newton John. The list goes on and on, from a pioneering daughter duo to a trailblazing of musical geniuses. There were 42 bands. It was a wave of musicians. He wouldn't write about all of them, only a few.

Elvis Presley was an American singer, rebel, and good actor. A talented genius and dubbed the "King of Rock and Roll" He has been regarded as on of the most significant culture figures for centuries. He energized interpretations with a provocative performance style, combined with a potent mix of influence across America. It was a transformation era that led him to success.

Elvis was born in Mississippi and relocated to Memphis, Tennessee, with his family at 13 years of age. He began his music career in 1954, recording at Sun Records with a producer, and received wider attention. Presley was on rhythm with an acoustic guitar.

A lead guitarist Scotty Moore and Bill Black was also a pioneer of rock ability, an up-tempo backbeat that drove country music and Rhythm and blues.

Elvis was born in Mississippi and relocated to Memphis, Tennessee, with his family at 13 years of age. He began his music career in 1954, recording at Sun Records with a producer, and received wider attention. Presley was on rhythm with an acoustic guitar.

A lead guitarist Scotty Moore and Bill Black was also a pioneer of rock ability, an up-tempo backbeat that drove country music and Rhythm and blues.

He was an American singer, rebel, and good actor. A talented genius and dubbed the “King of Rock and Roll.” He is regarded as one of the most significant culture figures for centuries. He energized interpretations with a provocative performance style, combined with a potent mix of influence across America. It was a transformation era that led to his success.

In 1955, a drummer joined to complete the quartet, and RCA Victor acquired his contract, and Presley made his first single, Heartbreak Hotel. He would sell 10 million copies within a year. A series of network television appearances and chart topping records all contributed to a new popular sound of Rock and Roll.

Title VII of the Civil Rights Act of 1964 made job discrimination illegal. Yet the Federal Government agency created to enforce this law, the Equal Opportunity Commission, failed to act on behalf of women for most of the Sixties, instead focusing on minorities. Under pressure from women activists at the beginning of the 1970s, The EEOC finally began to help women workers by filing gender discrimination lawsuits against companies. Occupational barriers began to fall.

The U.S. Congress passed additional legislation prohibiting sex discrimination, and a tax deduction for childcare expenses for families were both parents worked was also granted. For the first time, women were admitted to military academies and Ivy League universities.

Of all the movements, women's liberation remained the most controversial and far-reaching. In the 1970s, women's groups tried to create a more open and nurturing society. To achieve this, they demanded and won access to male-dominated businesses and universities. Women also made inroads into politics at the local, state, and national levels. They became doctors, lawyers, teachers, nuns, scientists, writers, plumbers, dock workers, pilots, stockbrokers, and sports heroes. By breaking down employment barriers and expanding opportunities, women transformed the character of the American family.

In some ways, though, 1970s Conservatism and the economy continued to flourish. For example, the crusade to protect the environment from all sorts of assaults of toxic industrial wastes, started in places like Love Canal.

Highways took off during the 1970s, and Americans for the first time, Americans celebrated Earth Day in 1970. The Clean Air Act and The Clean Water Act followed two years later.

The oil crisis of the late 1970s drew further attention to the issue of conservation. There was a cartoon on Saturdays for kids, “Give A Hoot” Don’t Pollute.

Environmentalism became a concern in the 1970s, with debates about how to best control pollution and the effect that pollution had on the environment as a whole, whether it was nuclear, chemical, or anything else.

The Three Mile Island had a meltdown at a nuclear power plant in Pennsylvania on March 28th at 4 am. It was the most significant accident in U.S. commercial nuclear power plant history. On the international Nuclear Scale, it was rated a level 5 and an accident with wider consequences.

There were failures in the non-nuclear secondary system followed by a stuck open relief valve in the primary system that allowed large amounts of nuclear reactor coolant to escape.

The mechanical failures were compounded by the initial failure of plant operators, which was recognized as a loss of coolant accident. The failure of operators is attributed to the out-of-the loop performance problem. The procedures left operators and management ill.

During the event, it was also compounded by design flaws, including inconveniently arranged instruments and controls, the use of similar alarms, and a failure of the equipment to clearly indicate the coolant inventory level or the position of the stuck open PORV.

This accident crystallized anti-nuclear safety concerns among activists and the general public and resulted in new regulations for the industry. It has been cited as a contributor to the decline of a new reactor construction program, a slowdown that was already underway.

The partial meltdown resulted in regulations in the release of radioactive gasses and radioactive iodine into the environment. There were failures in the non-nuclear secondary system followed by a stuck open relief valve in the primary system that allowed large amounts of nuclear reactor coolant to escape. Mechanical failures were compound by initial human failures.

The three of us who hung around together were now going to Abington High School. Once again, we had to take a bus. Half the time, we were skipping school, driving around, or playing games. Blake didn't have an interest in learning; at some point, he was confused about life and what to do that he would sleep in class. Occasionally, a couple of us would meet up with others, and we would go behind the Bowling Alley and drink beer.

Once in a while, we would go to a bar and hang out, play music, and drink beer. They didn't care, or should it be said no one's I.D. was being checked. At this time, the legal age was 18 years of age. On other days, we would go to the beer mart and get cases for 5.00 dollars. Bring it back to Pennsylvania and drink it.

We were only 15 years of age getting served. Once in a while, Blake would go to the Hollywood Tavern with some guys from Hollywood and drink beer. The owner never carded anyone.

None of us were excelling in school. In fact, back then, there was gang fighting in the cafeteria. The Township is broken up into sections with different names. And a few from different areas would fight others from another area. One day, he got off the bus and walked into school, and there was a big fight going on.

The reality of going to Abington High School was coming to an end for a short period of time. A half year went by, and the few kids, including Blake, were missing more days than was recommended by the guidelines. A half year went by, and Blake and a few of his friends were getting Fs on their report card. And the other year went by in school with the same results. They flunked 9th grade. The summer was here now.

The Fair was coming around, and a new drug came out. They called it T Buzz or Match-Head. The old heads were talking about it, and it was going around the neighborhood. The drug was white, and perhaps straight T.H.C.? The rumor was all you had to do was a little bit, about the size of a match-head.

They said it made you feel like you were floating on air. A few of us from Rockledge and a small crew from Hollywood decided to get together and go down to the fair and try it.

Perhaps a week or two went by, and everyone got together at night time and headed to the fair in Fox Chase. One of the guys pulled out The T Buzz and gave everyone a small piece. It made you feel like you were floating on air, and perhaps it was an an illusion. Everyone was laughing and going on rides, and playing booth games. There were probably about eight of us. They spent a few hours there, and everyone went home. No one after that night saw that drug again on the streets for some unknown reason.

The summer was going by, and nothing was changing regarding partying. Hanging out in the Dungun, that's what everyone called it. We would go up to Bill's house with his older brother, playing darts, and drinking beer. A couple of brothers would stop over from Hollywood, and that always led to playing Table Tennis and listening to music, usually Rock and Roll. They played a lot of Table Tennis and darts in the summer.

Reality was coming, and the summer was ending. Most likely, Blake thought about going back to school after failing 9th grade; that's when he got some news from his friend going to an Academy.

His father wanted a better life for his youngest son because he saw more intelligence in him. Their two elders, or the oldest, got a degree in business and worked for a big oil company got into the gas station and vice business, and a dry cleaners property in Blue Bell Montgomery County PA.With families in the neighborhood, his resources for workers were available.

The father knew he was bright because, at 15, his dad was teaching him to read Blue-Prints and could estimate construction management.

His dad decided to send him to Carson Long. When Blake found out, he asked his mom if he could go, and she said yes.

Carson Long Military Academy was in New Bloomfield, Pennsylvania, and was the oldest operating College preparatory boarding school and Military academy in the United States with Military training for boys in grades 9-12.

Carson Long Military Academy was founded in 1836 as Bloomfield Academy as a Latin Grammar school. In 1914, the United States of Colleges and Schools was also a member of the Association of Military Colleges.

The Cadets of Carson Long Military Academy were required to complete 21 credits for graduation. English, Math, Social Studies, History, Geography, Science and Mechanical drawing. Some Electives were public Speaking, Political Science, Combat Training and Martial Arts.

Physical Education and ROTC training were required for all cadets. At this time, the Cadets were not assigned a Military rank, they had to earn it, and the military rank system provided inspiration to allow students to aspire to leadership positions. The Cadet Corps was organized into a battalion of three companies. The cadet officers, under the guidance of the facility, were responsible for the performance of their companies, including discipline, appearance of formations, parades, and ceremonies. This peer leadership, along with faculty members is designated an honor school by the Department of Army. They offered advanced placement in math, sciences, and foreign languages. Cadets could also participate in junior and varsity sports, such as football, soccer, track, and field and rifle team, MP and Rangers. At that time, they had the M16. Blake entered the Academy. At first you were challenged by the new surroundings and structure.

They were Two-man rooms on two floors. Once you were settled in, you were handed a manual and an M16. The original M16 rifle was a 5.56×45mm automatic rifle with a 20-round magazine. Rifle, Caliber 5.56 mm, M16Barrel length: 20 in (508 mm)

The effective firing range is 550 m (601 yds.) (point target). The maximum firing range is 3,600m (3,973 yds.) And the rate of fire: 45–60 rounds/min semi-automatic

You were across from one another with single beds and wooden stand-up cubby hole shelves at the end of your bed with a desk between them.

Every morning, you wake up early and, cleaned your room, and make your bed. Inspection was done to your room by a senior Cadet.

Battalion formation was called every morning for announcements and inspection and to raise The flag with a salute. There were all types of people there with different personalities from just about all over America.

But it came down to one thing, and that is the Parents wanted to have their children a structure, and a better Education. However, you had young adults who could not get into the program. Once the Inspection came, you were off to classes in History, Science, Math, English, and Latin, and public speaking. Platoon inspection along with a battalion parade. The Rifle and Drill team, MP's, and Ranger recon were all available. Blake decided right away to get with the program, Academics, 7 days a week. You had a little bit of time during the day because you had other structural issues that had to be done. When dinner formation was over, you had the opportunity to seek the knowledge or, should I say, study.

Some people didn't take it seriously and couldn't maintain it. Therefore, they were dismissed, but for the most part, it was a time when you had an opportunity to make something out of yourself> The school was purchased by Theodore Long, a graduate of Bloomfield Academy and Yale who became a prominent Lawyer in Chicago. He named it in memory of his son, who died in a logging accident. It was a nonprofit governed by a board of trustees. Carson long has been accredited by their leadership and program.

In a way, he got lucky; his roommate was a Sergeant from South Philadelphia and was a good example and new the ropes in and out.

The first thing he did was started to crackdown on the schoolwork.

There were no T.V. Phones and or a computer. Going along with the program, shoes shined, buckle shined, and very well presented. The room and bed had to be in tip top shape, especially the bed neatly made with Army corners.

You go to the chow hall, and after that, you started your classes: English, Math, Science, Public Speaking, History, and Latin, and Mechanical drawing for some.  Classes were held in your building and others. Every building had a Military veteran as a teacher and role model. There was a Lieutenant who taught classes. I think he was R.O.T.C. and had a college education out of Bloomsburg, Pa.  The Kernel ran the school with a Major.

The building Blake was in had an old Korean War Veteran, a Captain. He gave you 1,300 pages of a book of American History and said read this, that was also 6 inches thick that went back to early history and up to the present time. You were getting tested, and there was no cheating. He was also the Latin Teacher. We would go down to the first floor for class.

Every one of us, as a child of his age for some, cannot get out of it. He is in a stream and swept along with it. All of his Sciences and study come to him out of it. Perhaps the tide will be changed. Our experience will absorb the efforts to change and take them into it as new trivial components, and the great movement of tradition and work will go on.

Once in a while, the cadets got the Captain going on the Korean War. O' yes, he would tell you the story. North Korea and the Soviet Union divided the 38th parallel into two Zones of occupation.

North Korea military forces crossed the border and drove into South Korea. Russia and China backed up North Korea in an invasion of South Korean 1950 to July 27th, 1953. It was all about the 38th parallel. It wasn't long after that China supplied troops to North Korea. America took forces with South Korea.

The United Nations Security council denounced the North Korean the move as an invasion and authorized the formation of the United Nations Command and the dispatch of forces to Korea to repel it.

The Soviet Union was boycotting the U.N. for recognizing Taiwan (Republic of China) as China, and China on the Mainland was not recognized by the U.N. No, the U.N. did not back it up but and make no mistake about it Americans Occupied 90% of forces.

After the first two months of the War, the South Korean army and American forces hastily dispatched to Korea were on the point of winning, breaking through the 38th parallel. Only the American President at the time wanted to retreat to a small area behind a defensive line known as the Pusan Perimeter.

A risky counteroffensive was launched, cutting off KPA troops and supply lines in South Korea. U.N. forces invaded North Korea in October and moved toward China. However, the Chinese People's Volunteer Army entered the War. The U.N. retreated from North Korea after the first and second phases. Chinese's forces were in South Korea by December.

Soul was captured four times, and communist forces pushed back to the 38th parallel. After this, the front stabilized, and the last two years were a War of attrition. The War in the air was never a stalemate. North Korea was subject to American Bombing attacks. Jet fighters confronted one another-in-airto-air combat, and Soviet pilots covertly flew in defense of their allies.

The Korean War was one of the most destructive conflicts of the modern era, with approximately 3 million war fatalities and a large civilian death toll. There were thousands of communist killings by the South Korean government and the torture and starvation of prisoners of War by North Korea. Additionally, several million South Koreans are estimated to have fled South Korea over the course of the War.

The war lasted for three years, and then the Korean Armistice Agreement was signed. The agreement created the (DMZ) to separate North and South Korea and allow returning prisoners. However, no peace treaty was ever signed.

Korea was technically still at war. Politicians were concerned about another World War. Or perhaps a communist campaign, people were calling it.

Japan annexed Korea, where it ruled for 35 years until the surrender of WWII in 1945.

Americans have been fighting Communism since WWI.

In WWII, General Patton wanted to take Russia. Winston Churchill recommended that Patton go through France and cut the Russians off and perhaps up to Russia to fight the Germans and Russia, who were running out of fuel, men and ammunition. Patton wanted to go on and take Russia. Washington wouldn't let him. He felt his destiny was to fight the greatest War in the World.

Some Scholars believe General Patton should have taken Russia because he said we are going to end up fighting them eventually.

According to most Historians, though the conflict in Southeast Asia had its roots in the French colonial period of the 1800s. The United States, France, China, Soviet Union, Cambodia, Laos, and other countries would, over time, become involved in the lengthy War North and South Vietnam were not reunited as one country. The following Vietnam War timeline is a guide to the complex and military issues that would ultimately claim lives.

The Academy was going well with morning room inspections and line ups. Shoes had to be spit-shined and your buckle polished. Classes and studying during the week kept you focused. History was one of his favorites, Latin was hard and one of the most complex subjects.

Latin, or Latinum: was a classical language belonging to the Italic Branch of the European languages. Latin was spoken in the lower Tiber area than known as (Latium) around present-day Rome and became the dominant language throughout Rome. Latin remained the common language of international communication, science, scholarship of academia, and political usage in Europe until the 18th century, and it eventually became a dead language in the modern linguistic definition.

Math was no joke; people took different reactions to Algebra, exploring how to use letters (called variables) and numbers with mathematical symbols to solve problems that also included evaluating expressions, witting equations and graphic functions, solving quadratics, and understanding inequalities.

He studied the schoolwork every day and on the weekends reading the material over and over again. It was the only way he could understand. Some people have a knack for understanding better than others.

So, every day, he would go and learn and look forward to the weekends. There would be an occasional walk up the mountain.

Blake started reading car magazines in some spare time. He was at the age when he could get a driver's license. It was just a thought. There were all types of cars out there with 4,6 and 8-cylinder engines. The seventies already had the two--barrel carburetors. However, there were four barrels was coming up. Some people modified their cars. Some cars could do 0 to 60 in 7 seconds. These cars were all metal, some with roll-down windows and some with power. They usually came with an AM FM radio or an eight-track until the cassette tape cams out.

These are the top muscle cars of the 70s

The 1977 Pontiac Firebird

The, 1970 Chevrolet Cheval

The 1978 Lil Red Express

The 1974 Pontiac Firebird Trans Am 455.

The 1970 Buick GSX

The 1970 Oldsmobile 442

So Blake figured he would just keep reading the school work over and over to learn on his own and pound it in his head. English was also one of his hardest subjects. Science was not difficult. There were no tutors at this time.

And it started paying off before he knew it; he was making 2nd honors in the class, and the piers were happy and wanted to promote him. There were two people ahead of him, one junior scientist and another who grew up on a farm reading books. Blake would laugh, while he would sit in front of him and sleep.

They let him, he was an A student. And that became privileges that no one else had, and 2nd honors got the same treatment. Blake went on Covert Military operations with Airborne forces are ground combat units carried by aircraft and airdropped into battle zones, typically by parachute drop. Parachute-qualified infantry and support personnel serving in airborne units are also known as paratroopers.

The main advantage of airborne forces is their ability to be deployed into combat zones without land passage, as long as the airspace is accessible. Formations of airborne forces are limited only by the number and size of their transport aircraft; a sizeable force can appear "out of the sky" behind enemy lines in merely hours if not minutes, an action known as vertical envelopment.

Airborne forces typically lack enough supplies for prolonged combat and so they are used for establishing an airhead to bring in larger forces before carrying out other combat objectives. Some infantry fighting vehicles have also been modified for Para dropping with infantry to provide heavier firepower.

Protocol I of the Geneva Conventions protects parachutists in distress, but not airborne troops. Their necessarily-slow descent causes paratroopers to be vulnerable to anti-air fire from ground defenders, but combat jumps are at low altitude (400–500 ft) and normally carried out a short distance away (or directly on if lightly defended) from the target area at night. Airborne operations are also particularly sensitive to weather conditions, which can be dangerous to both the paratroopers and airlifters, and so extensive planning is critical to the success of an airborne operation.

Advances in VTOL technologies (helicopter and tiltrotor) since World War II have brought increased flexibility, and air assaults have largely been the preferred method of insertion for recent conflicts, but airborne insertion is still maintained as a rapid response capability to get troops on the ground anywhere in the world within hours for a variety of missions.

Violent covert operations include a sabotage, assignation, and paramilitary support of armed insurgency against the opposing power.

C.I.A. activities were operations conducted by the Central Intelligence Agency. Blake participated in both the military and political aspects of the war The C.I.A. provided suggestions for political platforms, supported candidates, used agency resources to refute electoral fraud charges and manipulated the certification of election results. Blake worked particularly closely with ethnic minority and took enemy prisoners of war, and conducted rescue operations to retrieve prisoners of war, and conducted clandestine agent team activities and physiological operations.

Christmas vacation was coming around. For some, they did not go home and be with their families. Most of us were all looking forward to it.

It was time Blake and his friend got on the train to go to the 30th St. Train station. From there, they got on more trains, and before they knew it, they were home.

People in the neighbor looked upon you with a little respect coming home in a Uniform. It was just a big party, and in fact, it was time to go back. It was the same procedure once we got near the 30th St Train station, we had a few drinks. While on the train, his friend confessed he was going to smuggle an ounce of pot in. We arrived after dinner and it felt good to get a break.

Weekends were opportunities for weekend passes and for Military exercises, Drill Team, Parades, and Rifle training, studying, and free time. And, of course, your M16 had to be cleaned. You could go up the mountains for solitude or lounge around. In fact, there was a spring of water you could drink right out of the ground.

His friend told someone in his building he had pot, and he told, and they threw him out. His father was very unhappy about it. Blake was not involved, but he knew he sneaked it in.

Once a year, they had The Presidential Physical Fitness program, and it was coming soon. Calisthenics were an everyday thing.

He passed only from encouragement from others. The Academy and the staff took pride in building leaders, integrity, and honesty in young Americans along with The Armed Forces, The land of the Free from the Brave. Parents would come and watch us perform parades, Rifle drills, and other activities.

We could spend time with them and take pictures with family members. I believed it was a good thing to learn in a pattern of organization for the purpose of building leaders.

He knew it and saw something different. He felt proud to be a part of something he was good at. When you come from somewhere, and you're poor, and you see others doing good around you, what do you see for yourself? You admired the Platoon leaders and the Battalion leaders. They had the sabers.

He started to know people in the building and or class. Some took it more seriously than others. Perhaps everyone had a different story. There were some that came from well off families and others who had trouble affording it.

And there were also people who came from a higher class. It didn't matter where you came from. It was all about the military and leaders making good, productive members of society if you were willing.

It certainly was more advanced than a public school. It was a daily structured routine of cleaning and making your bed, and your appearance was expected to be neatly uniformed. Your tie had to be right and or be dressed uniformly. Every morning there was an inspection of your room and appearance for Platoon formation.

Blake was asked if he could memorize and stand in front of hundreds of people and recite the Gettysburg Address from his peers.

He told his superiors he can do it, and when the time came, he did it. He was nervous with hands that were sweating, looking straight ahead in front of hundreds of people wondering if he was going to forget something. From what he said to me, he felt nervous on the podium, looking at everyone and my peers. But he gave it a chance.

Blake stood up and delivered President Lincoln's Gettysburg Address that was on November 19, 1863, on the battlefield near Gettysburg, Pennsylvania. "Fourscore and seven years ago, our forefathers brought fourth, on this continent, a new nation, conceived in liberty and dedicated to the proposition that all men are created equal. Now we are engaged in a great civil war, testing whether that nation or any other so conceived and so dedicated can long endure.

We are met at a great battlefield of the war. We have come to dedicate a portion of that field as a final resting place for those here who gave their lives that that nation might live. It is altogether fitting and proper that we should do this.

But in a large sense, we cannot dedicate, we cannot consecrate-we cannot hollow-this ground. The Brave men, living and dead, who struggled here have consecrated it far above our poor power to add or detract.

The world will little note. Nor long remember what we say here, but it can never forget what they did here. It is for us the living rather to be dedicated here to the unfinished work that they who fought here have thus far so nobly advanced. It is rather for us to be here dedicated to the great task remaining before us—that from these honored dead we take increased devotion to that cause for which they here gave the last full measure of devotion—that we here highly resolve that these dead shall not have died in vain—that this nation, under God, shall have a new birth of freedom, and that government of the people, by the people, for the people, shall not perish from the earth."

Blake delivered The Gettysburg address, and everyone smiled. The crowed rose up and clapped. He did feel a sense of accomplishment even though he was unsure he was able to do Public Speaking.

The week was going by, and everyone was talking about maneuver warfare. We were going on the weekend and staying a week. Company A Verses Company B. It was a vast property of 200 acres of woodland environment.

The use is for initiative, discipline, loyalty, and a purpose for direction, and the use of the unexpected is combined with intelligence for determination to succeed.

Seek opponent's strengths while exploiting their weaknesses and attacking their critical superior force with mass to achieve physical destruction. Maneuvers are preemption, deception, dislocation, and disruption to destroy the enemy's will and ability to fight.

Blake felt a sense of accomplishment, even knowing he was unsure he could pull it off. The week was going by, and everyone was talking about the maneuvers that were coming this weekend. Before everyone knew it was time to go.

It was company A Against Company B you were backpacked with (UGR), and that is a United States military ration that is used by the Armed Forces and Department of defense.

It is intended to sustain groups of American service members with access to the kitchen field, serving as both a field ration and a garrison ration.

It is a of several older alphabetized rations namely the A-ration, B-ration and T-ration that combine them under a unified system. U.G.R. is designed to meet the military daily recommended when averaged over a 5 to 10-day period.

We were on our way on a five-mile run to the location and loaded up, including the M-16, rations, and a canteen of water to a 200-acre wooded lot. Finally, we arrived, and the first thing we had to do is make shelter. It did not take us long to make a shelter out of trees that were set up in a tri-pod formation.

What's next is now maneuver warfare; it is the use of initiative with originality and the unexpected, combined with determination to succeed. We covered eighty miles in 8 hours and finally discovered their location.

We had to seek our opponent's strengths while gathering their intelligence of their weaknesses for their critical vulnerabilities and the conceptual opposite of attrition warfare. Rather than seeking victory by applying superior force and mass to achieve physical destruction, Maneuvers uses perception, deception, dislocation, and disruption to destroy the enemy's will and ability to fight. Blake and Company B were sheltered and dug in.

Historically, maneuver warfare was stressed by small militaries, who were more cohesive, better trained, or more advanced in technology than their attrition warfare counterparts.

The term tactical maneuver" is used by maneuver warfare theorists to refer to movement by forces to gain an "advantageous position relative to the enemy" as opposed to its use in the phrase "maneuver warfare." The idea of using rapid movement by forces to gain is as old as war itself.

Blake's Company sheltered about twenty-five miles in on the right of the perimeter, and by now, it was 1300 hrs., and it was time for our rations.

After that, we had a small break while the platoon leaders, squad leaders, and the Platoon Sergeant were plotting a takeover. Time was going and we were ready to go fishing.. There was a creek nearby with some good trout and bass.

You had to make your own fishing pull, but they provided everyone with string. Everyone was off, and worms were the bait.

All three squads went out and were talking about our mission. There were some who thought Company A was in 80 miles deep in the woods.

The platoon had to find them before Company A found them. Others were talking about the Drill Team exercise coming soon. Everyone spent some hours fishing and it was 1600 hrs. and time to prepare dinner.

There were about 16 fish that were caught, and dinner was on the way for everyone. They also had natural spring water nearby, so there was plenty of water.

After dinner, everything was cleaned up, and the Platoon was getting ready for bed. They had to rise and shine at 0600. 0600 came, and everyone washed up, and camouflaged, and started on the move. Everyone was spread out about a foot apart, moving up the right side. The Platoon leader had an idea that Company A was about 21 miles in and on the East Side. He wanted to get near and gather their position. One person from each squad advanced ahead with radio gear and binoculars. The platoon was under strict command to use hand signals, no talking.

Sometimes, it's better to use hand signals which are agreed gestures or shapes that people make to communicate. "I want to speak," Look in that direction," I agree, "I don't understand," and etc. Using the signals can make things run more smoothly.

In six hours, Company B covered over 40 miles and saw nothing. Hours and miles went by until their headquarters was discovered. The scouts found them and reported back. It was also radio silence now, with their location and movement was being documented. Their squads were out, and there was no sight of them.

For a few more hours, the Company was gathering intelligence. And then everyone was told to relocate south, about 25 miles away in four hours.

Once we arrived, we had to make a new shelter just in case of rain, however, rain was not in the forecast for the week. We arrived and did what we had to and prepared ourselves for rations. There was talk that the leaders were developing a plan for attack.

The military science of commanders is to construe the large scale from the small scale, like making a monumental icon from a miniature model.

Such matters are hard to write about in detail; to know myriad things by means of one thing is a principal of military science. Blake's Company had to get up at 0100 hours.

This went on for a few days, getting as close to them as possible without being recognized. When you're fighting adversaries and get to feeling snarled up in maneuvers, remember the rule of military science: while in the midst of minute, suddenly shift to a large perspective.

Changing to great or small is an intestinal part of the science of the art of war. It is essential for warriors to seek this even in the ordinary conscious of human life. This mentality is critical to military science, whether large or small scale. This should be given careful consideration.

The Platoon leader knew his soldiers and was familiar in times of conflict after having reached the mastery to which one aspires. Having attained the power in the knowledge of the arts of war, you think of your own soldiers, understanding them as you wish, intending to command them freely. He is a commander, and the opponents were the troops also. This takes work.

Letting go of the hilt" has various meanings. It has a meaning without a shot fired and also has a meaning of failing to win if a shot is not fired. The various different senses cannot be written down but called for through training and practice.

Upsets happen in all sorts of things. One way it happens is being under acute pressure. Another is through a feeling of unreasonable strain. A third is through a feeling of surprise.

For the art of war to be real science, such as winning victory in battle with adversaries, no change whatsoever is to be made in these principles.

When you attain the power of my military science and put it into practice in a straightforward manner, there can be no doubt of victory.

In the course of the struggle for victory by military science, you also win by disrupting their defenses, by making moves opponents that don't expect, confusion, or irritating them, or scaring them, sensing the patters of the rhythm when opponents get mixed up.

It was day five, and the surprise attack was underway at 0100 hours. When the Platoon arrived they were captured under a surprise attack at 0500.

Everything thing was a good learning experience, and this was a good one. Everyone headed back to headquarters and ate; and some stayed up, and some went to bed.

The following day it was time to go back and prepare for The Rifle Drill team to put on an exhibition or ceremony in another week. Blake was on the team, and everyone had to demonstrate the types of command in a drill team.

Many drill procedures used by the Army were developed during the Revolutionary War. The purpose of the drill then was to install discipline in American soldiers. As these soldiers. As these soldiers mastered the art of the drill, they began to work as a team and develop a sense of pride in themselves and in their unit. In today's Army, the same objectives are implemented. Teamwork, confidence, pride, alertness, attention to detail, and discipline are accomplished by drill.

A drill consists of a series of movements by which a unit or individuals are moved in an orderly, uniform manner from one formation to another unit or individuals in an orderly, uniform manner from one formation to another or from one place to another. Units vary in size, but in basic combat training, you will ordinarily be part of a squad, section, platoon, or company.

First, you were taught the following drill terms;

Element: This is an individual, squad, section, platoon, or a larger unit formed as a part of the next higher unit.

Formation: This is an arrangement of the unit's elements in a prescribed manner, such as a line formation, in which the elements are side-by-side, and column formation, in which the elements are one behind another. In a platoon column, the members of each squad are one behind another with the squads abreast.

Front: This is a space from one side to another side of the formation and includes the right and left elements.

Depth: This is a space from the front to the rear of a formation, including the front and rear elements.

Distance: This is the space between elements that are one behind the other. The distance between individuals is an arm's length plus 6 inches, or approximately 36 inches, measured from the chest of one soldier to the back of the soldier immediately to his or her front.

Interval: This is the space with side by-side elements.

Rank: This is a line that is only one element in depth.

File: This is a column that has a front of one element.

Guide: This is the person responsible for maintaining the prescribed direction and rate of march.

Post: This is the correct place for an officer and noncommissioned officer to stand in the prescribed formation.

Head: This is the column's leading element.

Base: This is the element around that was planned or regulated.

Cadence: This is a uniform rhythm or number of steps or counts per minute.

Quick time: This is the cadence of 120 counts (steps per minute).

Double Time: This is a cadence of 180 counts (steps per minute).

The drill commands were oral orders by the commander or leader, usually in two parts. The preparatory command states the movement is to be carried out and gets you ready to execute the order. The command of execution tells when the movement is to be carried out. In the command is "Forward March," the preparatory command is "Forward," and the command of execution is "March."

In some commands, the preparatory command and the execution were combined, for example, "fall in" "At ease," and "Rest'. These commands are given without infliction and at a high pitch comparable to that of a normal command execution.

The command was given Fall in and attention, and our weight was equally distributed equally on the heels and balls of your feet.

When we came to attention, our weight was distributed smartly with your toe's forming a 45-degree angle. Keep your legs straight without locking your knees. Held our body erect with the hips level, your chest lifted, and your shoulders square and even. Your arms should be straight but not stiff, with the backs of your hands outward. Your fingers were curled in so that the tips of our thumbs were alongside and touching the first joint of the fingers. Everyone's thumbs were straight and along the seams of your trousers. The first joint of our forefingers was touching the seams. Keep your head up, and look straight to the front.

Parade rest was the next command only from the position of attention. On the command of execution "Rest" we moved our left foot 10 inches to the left of your right foot, keeping your legs straight without locking your knees. At the same time, you move your feet and place your hands at the small of your back, centered on your belt. Keep the fingers of both hands extended and joined, interlocking your funds. So that the palms of your right hand are outward. Hold your head up straight and look straight to the front. Once at the position of ease, we stood at ease, or rest maybe commanded from this position.

The next command of execution was "About Face. "Face" Everyone touched their toe of their right foot to the ground about half about half the length of your foot to the rear and slightly left of the left heel. Everyone rested their left foot weight on the heel and alloyed your knee to bend naturally. On the second count, we turned 180 degrees to the right on the left heel and on the ball of the right foot, resuming the position of attention. Hold your arms at attention when executing this movement.

The next command was the “(Hand Salute)” “Present arms.” on the command of execution, everyone rose their right hand sharply, fingers and thumbs extending and joined, palm facing down, and placed the tipped right forefinger on the rim of their visor slightly to the right of their right eye The outer edge of the hand is slightly downward so that neither so the back of the hand nor the palm is clearly visible from the front. The hand and wrist are straight, the elbow inclined slightly forward, and the upper arm is horizontal.

“Order, arms are a one-count movement from the hand salute. On that command of execution “Arms” the hand was returned sharply to the side, resuming the position of attention.

Forward march.” everyone shifted their right foot, striking the ground and, taking one step with your left foot and stepping off again with your left foot. This is executed without command until “Change step, march.

The command halt was given, and the platoon took one more step and then brought their trailing foot alongside your leading foot, resuming the position of attention.

The next step was marching in place or “mark time, march. When everyone heard that you brought the trailing foot alongside your leading foot you began marching in place. To do that each foot was raised alternately two inches off the ground, and your arms continued to swing naturally.

All soldiers must be able to execute the drill movements called the manual of arms with the M16 rifle, both at the halt and while marching.

No one carried their magazine while marching. If you are performing a duty that requires the use of the magazine, carry the weapon at sling arms.

We assumed order arms at parade rest on hearing the command of execution of "Attention" "Order arms" are the position of attention with the rifle. The butt of the weapon was centered on your right foot, with sights to the rear. The toe of the butt should touch your foot so the rear sight and pistol grip form a line straight to the front.

The weapon is held with your right hand in a U formed by extending your joined fingers and thumb. Hold the weapon above the sight, with the right thumb, and of execution, "Arms" everyone grasped their barrel with the right hand and raised hand forefinger pointed downward and on line with the flat surface of the hand guard. The team kept their right hand and arm behind the rifle so that your thumb was along the seam of your trousers.

Everyone assumed the rest position with the rifle the same as you would without it, plus the following steps.

On the command "Parade rest" everyone grasped the barrel with their right hand and thrusted the muzzle forward, keeping the right arm straight, and then stood at ease with their head and eyes toward the commander.

Port arms from at ease is a two-part movement. The command was given "Port arms" "On the rifle diagonally across the body, keeping the elbow down. With the left hand, simultaneously grasp the hand guard just forward of the slip ring so that the rifle is about 4 inches from the belt. On the second count, everyone re-grasped the rifle at the small of the stock with the right hand. The rifle was held diagonally across the body about four inches from the belt, with the right forearm horizontal and the elbows close to the sides.

Present Arms was the next demonstration. On the command of execution, "Arms" was executed and port arms were in two counts. On the third count, everyone twisted their rifle with the right hand so that the magazine well was to the front and moved the rifle to a vertical position with the carrying handle about 4 inches in front of and centered on the body. Lower the rifle until the left forearm is horizontal; keep the elbows in at the sides.

The command was given, "Inspection arms" "On the command of execution, "Arms," they executed port arms in two counts. On the third count, you moved your left hand from the hand-guard and grasp the pistol grip, thumb over the lower portion to the bolt catch.

On the fourth count, the grip was released, unlocking the charging handle with the thumb and sharply pulling the charging handle to the rear with the thumb and forefinger. At the same time, apply pressure on the lower portion of the bolt catch, locking the bolt to the rear.

On the fifth count, without changing the grasp of the right hand, push the charging handle forward until it is locked into position. Then re-grasp the rifle with the right hand at the small of the stock. On the sixth count, everyone was removing their left hand and twisted the rifle with the right hand so that the injection port was skyward. Re-grasp the hand-guard with the left hand just forward of the slip ring and twisted the rifle so that the sights were up and the Platoon leader was visually inspecting the receiver through the injection port. And then twist the rifle so the sights are up.

"Ready, port, arms" is the only command given from inspection arms. On the command "Ready" move the left hand and re-grasp the rifle with the thumb and the fingers forming a U at the magazine well and trigger guard, and with the thumb without pressure on the upper part of the bolt catch. On the command "Port" press the bolt catch and allow the bolt to go forward. With the fingertips, push forward and close the dust cover. Grasp the pistol grip with the left hand and, place the left hand, and place the left thumb on the trigger. On the command "Arms," pull the trigger and resume arms.

The command is "Right shoulder; "arms" On the command of execution, "Arms" grasp the barrel of the weapon with the right hand and raise it diagonally across the body. With the left hand, grasp the hand-guard just in front of the slip ring. On the second count, everyone released the barrel with the right hand and grasp the butt, positioning the rifle. Twist the rifle and place it on the right shoulder. At the same time, move the left hand to the small of the stock and, guide the weapon to your shoulder, and then move your left hand back to attention. What a drill with an enormous amount of concentration, everyone was glad that it was over.

Two nights a week for practice was mandatory after dinner for two hours. Academics were going well with the week going by quickly. Before everyone knew it, it was Saturday, and the Parade was coming out on the field.

Saturday was here, and at 1800 hours, the Battalion was on the field.                For a military parade. The stands were full, and the Kernel and the Major were out. Today, it will be used to demonstrate discipline and cohesion in a modern military force.

Today, military parades include all aspects of military drill, from an exhibition drill of precision drill teams and military bands (in addition to the occasional corps of drums and drum and bugle corp. When on parade, most of the participating soldiers wear their ceremonial uniforms and carry the standards/colors of their respective.

The Battalion or the three Platoons were in formation in at ease. A Military. position assumed by a soldier or sailor in which the feet are 12 inches (30.48 centimeters) apart, the hands are clasped behind the back, and the head is held motionless and facing forward. Can you speak at the parade rest?

Remain silent and do not move unless otherwise directed. Why do soldiers stand at parade rest?

Like "Attention' Parade Rest is a form of respect given to NCOs by those junior in rank. All personnel should immediately go to the position of "stand at-ease" until told to "carry-on". Fall in. Individuals form a formation at the position of attention.

Attention. ...

Present, Arms.

Order, Arms.

Open ranks, March.

Close ranks, March.

Dress right, Dress.

Today, the modern snare drum tends to act as the driving cadence for marching bands, and snare drums are still used in some military contexts to keep the soldiers marching in step and they keep everyone marching in step.

Marching refers to the organized, uniformed, steady walking forward in either rhythmic or route-step time, and, typically, it refers to overland movements on the foot of military troops and units under field orders.

The end of the term was near and accommodations and or promotions were being given out. Some people haven't seen their family for a year, before he knew it, the year was over, and his mother was on her way up to take him home. Some people say all good things come to an end. He was disappointed and was not able to go back.

His mother asked for assistance for help from her brother to send him back. He said no and decided to send his own son to a more elite Academy; what a waste of money they threw him out.

Blake also went over to the house across the street to say hello to everyone.

It was an old wooden house. They lived on an acre lot. I was friends with brothers and a sister growing up. The oldest brother was in Vietnam, and it took a toll on him. The other two played and tinkered with cars at an early age. The youngest brother joined and made a career out of the Navy as a civil engineer. The father died at an early age, but the mother was a humbly strong woman who supported four children being a waitress.

Blake started contacting the kids his age up the street. Their family had a masonry business doing work in Blue Bell.

There were developments being built for the well-off. The father, who everyone called (Pop) liked a few beers after work and saw nothing wrong with it. We all started drinking.

During the summertime, we knew a family from Hollywood, and we get together and shoot pool and or go behind the bowling Alleys and have a few bears. There were other families with kids we hanged around with.

Blake would occasionally also go up the street and play table tennis and darts and have a few beers. His friend was the youngest of four brothers, and he was working for another brother doing Mechanics.

Sometimes, there were others who his brother knew, and they were hanging up at The Huntingdon Valley Shopping center. There was a Pool hall, a Bowling alley, an ice cream shop, and/or a strip mall.

Everyone could get in the Pool Hall and shoot pool and play Pinball, and then It wasn't long after that, at 16 years of age, we were getting served in The Hollywood tavern and drinking behind the Bowling Alley. Becomes more popular. There was a little bit of wood behind it with a stream of water. People in the adjoining neighborhood would go behind it and meet to drink bear.

That summer, he took a job at the car wash for a few dollars an hour. There wasn't any other way if you wanted to earn money. Some of us started working at an early age to have spending money.

You could say drinking beer became a normal for people at a young age. At the era it seemed like there were more of a male population than female. Young kids hanged around or sided with others in the borough, and some of that extended out to Fox Chase and Hollywood.

That summer, Blake and his friend from up the street planned to go to the shore for the weekend with two girls from the neighborhood. Bill had bought a 69 olds delta 88 complete with all amenities. We took a trip down Wildwood with the girls and got a motel. They left the girls behind and left for a bar.

They stayed for a couple of hours and shot some pool. And then left on the way to the motel, a Taxi cab side-swiped the car, and they swerved into a concrete light pole.

Bill hit the windshield, and Blake got out and walked away. They arrested Bill, and Blake had to call for a ride home back to Pennsylvania. It was a ruined weekend for everyone. A lot of time was spent in the basement up the hill on Blake Ave.

Now, there was a small pool table in the living room, ping pong and darts were in the basement. The summer was going by. Occasionally, Blake would keep in touch with the neighbor down the street. He took us for rides up New Hope and The race track. Flemington Speedway was in Flemington, New Jersey.

It was a dirt track or what they called Stock cars. So many laps around the track, and a winner was named. They had concession stands, and there was food, beer, and a race on Saturday night. One of the neighbors on the street built his own Stock car and raced it.

Before Blake knew it he re-entered high school. Things were vague, he doesn't know if he skipped a grade or what happened, all he knew was his Academic (Transcripts) were like something they had never seen, they were so high they told him to stay in school and go to summer school, and they would graduate him.

Basically, they came to him with a very good deal, skipping a whole grade. He had tried for a couple of months to graduate but could not maintain. The science teacher tried to encourage him to stay.

All his friends were working and making money, and him being without money and being hungry. He quit school about three months later. His mom didn't care; in fact, she had a new boyfriend. He really wasn't a role model.

It's so hard to describe at this age and where you see where you're able to go. He started regressing back and thought again he didn't know anything about a purpose. Even at times his instinct Looked like a down role spiral. And or may have seen a conclusion he could not win or weigh his chances for success. Our Governor from 1971 until 1979 was for not hunger, poverty, desperation, and chaos in America. The seeds of totalitarian regimes are nurtured by misery and want.

The spread and grow in the evil soil of poverty and strife. I need not tell you, ladies and gentlemen, that the American situation was serious.

It was apparent to all intelligent people and to Blake to think one difficulty was the problem of T.V. Radio that was making it unclear the complexity of the situation for the man on the street to make a clear appraisement of his future. His Grandmother would tell him the T.V. was bad for people. Furthermore, people and politicians were distant from poverty families, and it was unheard of for them to comprehend the plight and consequences reactions of the long suffering. I took my first job working at a Restaurant for a dollar an hour, but that didn't last long.

He got a job cutting grass again for a few dollars an hour. A couple of the guys he knew from the area worked there, and they got him a job. He worked a season in the Landscaping trade.

After that he also decided to go to welding school, a 6-month government grant program. Blake couldn't weld, but he stuck with it and passed. It was horizontal, flat, overhead, and vertical. There were no jobs welding. It was a waste of time or some money scheme for funding. He didn't look at himself as a good welder. He really couldn't get the hang of the overhead, vertical, and flat. It was a free government program. They passed him anyway. But there were no jobs, really.

He took a job as a masonry laborer from a man up the street. His member of his family was an apprentice. You had to labor, set up scaffolds, make cement, and move hundreds of blocks a day for a couple of years before you got a Masonry apprenticeship.

Once the pier was made on each floor and or at the ends, the masons were laying 4 or 5 hundred 8inch, blocks a day, you had to keep them moving. Of course, sometimes things were different: stone fronts, bricks, and fireplaces. Developments of luxury homes were being built in a picturesque place. There was a rumor he was working for a builder who married someone in the syrup business. It was outside of Norristown, at the Capitol of Montgomery County. It was called Blue-Bell, all this farmland.

Every day, we walked up the street and, got in the back of the pickup truck, and drove 30 minutes, and go to work. The first thing you had to do was make cement, and load 8in or 12 in blocks, and build a scaffold. People wanted to move out of Norristown, which is plagued with violence, drugs, and crime.  Bluebell townships were all farmland and it was being sold off.

He had two sons as masons and a few more at times. He would give you a job and a trade in the neighborhood. There was a lot of building going on and abroad in the fifties, and sixties, seventies, and eighties. More and more land would become scarce. Blake saved up and bought his first vehicle. A sixty-eight Ford pickup 3 speeds on the column.

Blake and his friend took it out one night and were heading up to a bar on Old York rd. to make a pot deal. We didn't get very far; when the police pulled them over, they found a quarter pound of pot in the roof.

Blake was released, and his friend was driving so he got arrested. He doesn't recall what happened after that, but he knows his name was not mentioned. He lost the truck.

Cars were cheap, a couple of hundred dollars, you had to look for them and bargain. And it was easy to work on any of the motors, they were straight sixes or V eights. Volkswagens or the beetle were out promoting a gas saver.

Not all cars were stick shifts, but the change was here. Car manufacturers were coming out with automatics and gear shifts, power windows, and a cassette tape with an A.M.F.M radio. And bucket seats. Cars were made out of metal, not plastic. Once in a while he would go up to The Lincoln Drive and watch movies with other people and drink some beer. We would ride around and listen to music. The seventies were like a wave of music, mostly Rock, as you will read.

Born in Berkeley, California, Fogerty and his brother Tom organized the group that would become Creedence as the Golliwogs in the late '50s. As Creedence Clearwater Revival, they released nine Top Ten singles, all written by Fogerty, between 1969 and 1971, starting with the standard "Proud Mary." They also scored eight gold albums between 1968 and 1972, all fueled by Fogerty's simple, driving rock songs and his burly baritone, intoning deceptively poetic ("Bad Moon Rising") and even political.

As the singer/songwriter and guitarist for Creedence Clearwater Revival, John Fogerty created a monumental and mythic American music. Drawing equally from rockabilly, country, and blues -- all sounds associated with the South, a region far away from Fogerty's native Northern California -- Fogerty developed a distinctive brand of rock & roll and a formidable songbook. After CCR suffered an acrimonious split in 1972, Fogerty didn't run away from that sound, but he did avoid the band's hits due to a lengthy legal dispute with his former record label in a fight so nasty that it culminated with Fantasy Records suing the rocker for plagiarizing himself on "The Old Man Down the Road," a fight he'd win. "The Old Man Down the Road" is the Top Ten single that kicked off Fogerty's successful solo career. It arrived in 1985, a full decade after his last hit, "Rockin' All Over the World," but the song and its accompanying Centerfield album pushed him back into the spotlight. He continued to be a force on record and on the road, where he eventually worked old CCR tunes into his set lists.

Creedence split up in 1972. Fogerty at first confused his considerable following by releasing an album of covers under the name the Blue Ridge Rangers in 1973. This was followed by a formal solo album, John Fogerty, in 1975, and then silence for more than nine years while the artist worked out business problems with Creedence's old label. But Fogerty returns with a Top Ten single, "The Old Man Down the Road," and a number one album, Centerfield. Fogerty went into seclusion and bounces back. By this year, America multiplied good bands.

It's always nice riding up the country and listening to music on 232 that leads to New Hope. Blake and his friends would go for a walk stop and have a couple of beers. The River was there that separated Pennsylvania from New Jersey. And then there was driving over the Bridge to go to Roger Wilco and get a case of beer for 4.00 dollars and got to The Stock car races. And even stop at a local bar and have a few. 18 years of age was the legal limit, but people were getting served at 16. Even in bars in Philadelphia, they were serving underage minors. At his time, he started to become an alcoholic, just like his father. Drinking was almost an everyday and weekly thing.

Some pain pills came around the neighborhood, Rorer 714; it was said you took one of them and added a couple of beers, and you were knocked on your ass.

Evidently, The Government ruled it out because it was so strong. Even now, if you know the right people, 714 are on the Black market. The problem now with the Black market is you really don't know what you're getting. It's a risk that could cost you your life.

The 1970s also saw an initial increase in violence in the Middle East as Egypt and Syria declared war on Israel, but in the late 1970s, the situation in the Middle East was fundamentally altered when Egypt signed the Egyptian–Israeli Peace Treaty.

The seventies also saw The UNIBOMBER, the man that the world would eventually know, a man who came to our attention in 1978 with the explosion of his first primitive homemade bomb at a Chicago university.

Over the years, he mailed or hand-delivered a series of increasingly sophisticated bombs that killed three Americans and injured nearly two dozen more. Along the way, he sowed fear and panic, even threatening to blow up airliners in flight.

In 1979, an FBI-led task force that included the ATF and U.S. Postal Inspection Service was formed to investigate the "UNABOM" case, code-named for the University and Airline bombing targets involved. The task force would grow to more than 150 full-time investigators, analysts, and others. In search of clues, the team made every possible forensic examination of recovered bomb components and studied the lives of victims in minute detail.

These efforts proved of little use in identifying the bomber, who took pains to leave no forensic evidence, building his bombs essentially from “scrap” materials available almost anywhere. And the victims, investigators later learned, were chosen randomly from library research.

People felt confident that the Unabomber had been raised in Chicago and later lived in the Salt Lake City and San Francisco areas. This turned out to be true. His occupation proved more elusive, with theories ranging from aircraft mechanics to scientists. Even the gender was not certain: although investigators believed the bomber was most likely male, they also investigated several female suspects.

Anwar Sadat, President of Egypt, was instrumental in the event and consequently became extremely unpopular in the Arab world and the wider Muslim world. Political tensions in Iran exploded with the Iranian Revolution in 1979, which overthrew the authoritarian Pahlavi dynasty and established an even more authoritarian Islamic leadership of Ayatollah Khomeini.

Blake got into some trouble beating a man up. There were three of us down the street drinking. And an argument started over a girl, and the fight broke out. Apparently, his jaw was broken.

The next day, the Police came and knocked on the door for him. He slammed the door in their faces and ran upstairs. The Police ran around the back door, and he went upstairs to the front bedroom and, opened the window, and jumped out the window. He has been lost since he was a child, the Minister said to him.

A neighbor from up the street was coming down and put him in the back of his trunk. He was hiding out until someone made a phone call and was told where to go. At this point he was a wanted man by

Law Enforcement. He ended up making his way into the section of Olney in 1979. A man was running a small trash business out of his house. Did Blake get a break or a double-edged sword at the same time?

He was a single parent. The owner had started scraping at an early age until finally, he had bought a single axial Roll off truck that worked out of his house in North Philadelphia. There are metal dumpsters that are from 10, 15,16, 20, 25, 30, and 40 cubic yards. There used for trash, demolition, concrete, and whatsoever. This was just one type of this truck that's in the business.

The owner of the company bought a 1979 Mack truck, a Roll-Off 10-wheeler that is designed to pull up the containers onto the truck with Rails that rose up until the back of the rails touched the ground. Every load had to be manually tarpped and strapped down.

And then you raise the rails and hook up the cable to the dumpster and pulled it up to the front of the truck or perhaps put a stop on the rails and partly pull it up and snug it. You had to engage the Power take--off to engage the hydraulic system to pull up the container with a steel cable.

By the 1700s, refuse had become a major problem; waste was still dumped in the streets and open burning of garbage was a common practice. Dogs roamed freely, and the garbage overflowed. Benjamin Franklin supposedly started the first street cleaning service.

By the early 1800s, trash did not disappear, rather, it was everywhere that was accumulated over the decades from human habitation. Even the front yard of the typical home was a disgrace, consisting of an inlaid pavement of bones and broken bottles, the relics of departed earthenware, or the fragments of abandoned. It took over a hundred years before reports were linking disease to a filthy environment and that launched the age of Recycling.

Dick was his name and really flying under the radar in the business. He had some accounts and did well enough to buy a new 1979 Mack Truck. He offered to teach Blake at 4 dollars an hour. There are various types of Rubbish trucks.

In 1979 Dick took him out and showed him about the RPM to time and shifts the gears. A six-speed with a low gear. You started out in first gear. In some circumstances, you had to take up two lanes to turn. I recall the first time he took me to the N. J. Landfill over the Tacony Palmyra Bridge. For the first time, he had to drive over the Tacony Bridge. He was a little nervous in a big truck with cars beside him. A golden rule Blake was taught to stay a little more to the right or the white line. He had enough confidence and said yes. Let's do this. The turns had to be taken wide and, in some cases, taking up both lanes. He would take me out driving for about two weeks and observed me and wondered if he could do it. When you are driving a 10-wheel truck, you are taking on the responsibility of hauling sixty-four thousand pounds, G.V.W. Blake was ready, and at this time, the owner took him up to DMV for commercial vehicles. The owner told Blake he knew a State Trooper who worked at the State Police barracks in Nasheminy. He was now taking his written, Pre-trip, and road tests.

When we arrived at the State Police Barracks, he gave the officer a pre-trip inspection, and then he took him out for an hour. He felt somewhat nervous, but he also felt confident that he could be a good and safe driver. Blake always had a straight path that he would try and wanted to practice against dangerous situations and despite others' adverse conditions or the mistaken of others? Blake passes all the tests.

It cannot be achieved by adhering to general guidelines such as two or three seconds of a gap behind road rules and emergency situations and the basics of mechanical driving. He was a defensive driver constantly being aware of my surroundings.

He had one truck, and the other Refuse companies were watching him. There was a guy from Montgomery County who tried to come into the city and get trash. They rallied against him and forced him out of the city and into a landfill.

Before, Blake knew it, he was getting up early and working some nights and weekends, picking up dumpsters from companies and contractors; he had quit a few roofers, too. One contract was up on Benet Rd. He had for years. Blake was driving in and around.

He had three or four companies with fictitious names. He had him for years. Blake didn’t know what was going on up there; someone threw a propane tank through his front door. It wasn’t long after that he got indicted. There were rumors going around he was going on people's roofs and slicing them? Everything was going to the Landfills in New Jersey and, Pennsylvania, and Montgomery County.

At this time, Blake cut all his ties with neighborhood friends. The people he grew up on the street, Bill bought a house on the creek in

Feasterville and rebuilt it.

And gave up drinking and used to follow the Bible, but that didn't last long. I was trying to turn my life around, but I found myself lying and cheating all these people.

Blake worked out his House and garage, and he lived there for a year. Every week, I had to grease and wash the truck. He was keeping a well-kept secret to himself, and that was to buy the scrap yard up the road. Blake was about to get his Class B license. They took me in and showed me the ropes for a while.

The only thing he did was learning by watching. This was an opportunity for him and, at the same time, a double- edged-sword.

He had a daughter in College and another on the way and two sons that were in High school. He built some containers out of his garage.

The bigger companies didn't look at him as a threat. But little did they know perhaps he was the smartest one out of them all.

The Trash business was no joke: fire bombings, stealing stops and containers. You are competing with companies who had 20 plus trucks that were family businesses started by Grandfathers. Trash, Refuse, and Garbage are a never-ending commodity.

Every day he was waking up early and following a schedule he planned out for me. He had customers who were manufactures of vinyl products. He was driving around all day picking up and delivering dumpsters.

He would go to a few places at night to work the overtime, and started out making 4.00 dollars an hour. That year and that time the minimum wage was 4.25 cents an hour. He worked days and nights. He had a debt that he had to pay.

Every year, he would start asking for a dollar raise. Every Saturday, I would clean the truck inside it and out and grease it.

He told me a story one time about the first roll-off he bought, an old single Mack truck, and he never knew, or no one told him you had to grease all the fittings. If you don't do this, the parts wear down, and that's what happened, they broke. He was getting on his feet.

Blake had to get to know the customer's location and all around the city, including the troublesome neighborhoods and the Counties around the city and the states including New Jersey. He had to learn about the closest Landfills. He started in Cinnaminson Ney, Jersey, and Deptford, running trash over there. It was cheap to dump fifty cents a yard. You can dump anything in there.

The owner or boss had a problem with one of his customers. There was a Carpet Company that manufactured carpet, and the residual waste was a 50-gallon drum of Latex. It caused a problem at some landfills. He told the owner of the company to put the drum on the bottom of the 30-cu yard container and cover it up with carpet waste and whatsoever. Blake had to juggle it around to different places; no one really wanted it.

And twice a month, Blake would pick an old dilapidated container, perhaps a 16 cu yds. At a cemetery in North Philadelphia, even though they were told a twenty. Anyway, one day, he took it to the South Philadelphia transfer station. You had to pull up to a scale and hand him your credit card, and on the bell, you could pull off and go inside the building. The place was inside dark and dusty, with particles in the air, and then you had to drive in and pulled up and then back up as close to a curb before the deep pit and open your door. Pull back a little further to the curb and raise the rails. He looks in his mirror while powering down, and the overhead crane operator grabs his load while crushing it, and all these bones and ashes come out. He just left, and after that, he never looked in the mirror after that with that load.

He then moved into an apartment at Fifth St. in Olney. Blake took a one-bedroom apartment for a few hundred dollars a month. It was a diverse neighborhood. He didn't like the place; the neighborhood was dirty with trash.

Blake stayed there for a year living there. I was working nights running to N.J. and was dumping on some man's front yard, only for some reason, that didn't last long. He rented another apartment on 2nd and Fisher. He didn't like it there. The owner had other stops, a Vinyl company that he was giving them a can with the wrong size but charging them for something bigger.

That load was taken out to Montgomery County landfill and in the winter, most of the time digging the load out by hand. Frozen vinyl, but it wasn't long after that the trash guys were spraying the inside of the can with diesel fuel so the load would not stick to the metal. The work was coming in days and nights, working 60 hours a week.

He ran into an old friend from South Korea, an Asian; he had asked me to help him with his life. He left his wife and or family behind in South Korea. He wanted me to share an apartment with him and teach him English.

He was 55 years of age and a Master of the Martial Arts and Samurai. Blake took him up on his offer. He put the money up to share a two-bedroom apartment around the neighborhood.

Kim was born in Korea on December 11, 1935. He began his formal martial arts training at the age of four, instructed by his father and his uncle who were Grand Masters, to learn his family's martial arts system, a system based on stepping, spinning, and jumping, short stick, and samurai.

They had a rice pot, so I as was eating rice and Korean food all the time mixed with a few things. We discussed things and to understand his culture, it was essential to realize that no government has, ever united the whole country.

The Imperial government has always ruled the whole land in theory but never in fact. The leadership had never been more than a center of powerful factions competing with other powerful factions.

Things were mysterious. He had a friend who was in America. He promised him citizenship if he worked for him. The plan was the new master was going to take over the martial Arts Place with samara, short stick, and combat. They put the plan into action, and he asked me to assist him. Blake started from the bottom up.

The neighborhood wasn't the greatest. Mostly poor people, so the school never did really well. It gave him something to do at night that was constructive, and he also wanted to learn the English language. Blake started working-out five-times a week and competing.

The master carpenter knows the measurements and designs of all sorts of structures employees people to build. In this respect, the master carpenter is the same as the master warrior.

Efficiency and smooth progress, prudence in all matters, recognizing true courage and different levels of morality and installing what can and cannot be reasonably expected are the matters of the mind of the master carpenter. The principles of martial arts are like this.

There are three kinds of preemption. One is when you preempt by attacking an opponent on your own imitative; this is called preemption from a state of suspension. Another is when you preempt an opponent by making an attack on you; this is called preemption from a state of waiting. Yet another is when you and an opponent attack each other simultaneously; this is called preemption in a state of mutual confrontation.

These are the three ways of preemption. At the beginning of any battle, there are no other choices but these three initiatives.

Since it is a manor of gaining victory quickly by preemption, therefore preemption is the foremost concern in martial arts.

There are many details involved in preemption, but they cannot be fully written down because it is a matter of putting priority on the pattern of the particular time, perceiving the opponents, and using your knowledge to win.

When you want to attack, you remain calm and quiet, then get the jump on your opponent by attacking suddenly and quickly. You can preempt by outwardly and swiftly by leaving inwardly reserves. You can also get the jump by stealing your mind to the utmost accelerating you're pace a bit, and making a violent attack the instant you get up close to your opponent.

You can also let your mind go free, determining to beat your opponent at the same thing from start to finish, gaining victory by through going strength of heart. These are all examples of preemption from a state of suspension. The moves are hard to write about in detail; They should be worked out along the general lines of the moves written. Even though you are not to be always the one to attack, it's better to put opponents on the defensive. Four to six days a week for hours a day.

On a Saturday, Blake took the master to a high school field not far away. Blake didn't know it at the time what he was doing. We arrived, and he wanted to see how many seconds it would take me to run 100 yards.

What he was working on was speed; with speed, Blake was able to jump and leap forward in less than a second. After months of practice it was all coming together. It was inexpensive and a new experience, and it didn't hurt to help and learn something new. The Master's theory was speed is power.

Every day, he was also getting up early and working some nights and weekends, picking up dumpsters from companies and contractors; he had quit a few roofers, too. One contract was up on

Benet Rd. He had for years. Blake pulled a lot of old roofing material for years. The owner had a 30-yard container in his yard full-time. The workers were empting the stuff at the end of the day.

It wasn't long after that he got indicted. There were rumors going around he was going on people's roofs and slicing them? Everything was going to the Landfills in New Jersey and Pennsylvania and Montgomery County Landfills for years.

Some other different companies were getting a16 cubic yards for twenty or 25 for a thirty-yarder, and the landfills were told they were 15 Yards. Another landfill he was introduced to was in Bucks County. It was located right on the Delaware River. They had these huge Bulldozers with metal Spike tires.

Trucks were a mile long waiting to get into the Landfill to get in the morning. They were coming from all over. New York and New Jersey. And they were bringing in tractor-trailer loads.

They would take garbage, asbestos, chemicals, paper, and anything you could think of all day long. Everything was classified as trash until it was segregated into other categories.

Blake's first battle was the largest tournament in America at Madison Square Garden. He took the train up by himself and walked around for a while and then entered. Blake lost his first battle and went back home by train.

He started working out up at the school, and then one day and, he fell on his right arm and reinjured it. He had to go back into the hospital for surgery. The Tri-Sep tendon ripped apart again. They had to cut my elbow open again and repair it or try to attach it. He was out of work for a few days but he went back working with a cast on.

Blake was running refuse to a Recycled management company, that covered the fill or more else ran operations at the landfill? It was out in a place up in Bucks' County; however, things were vague and they were getting so big. By law, you were allowed 279 feet in the air.

There was so much money and political connections. They opened up another one down the street on the river. They were the largest in the world. You pulled up, went down a road, and were directed to other trucks lined up in a line to dump. In some cases, you had to be pulled back by the machine.

When it rained, it was like a marsh, stuff popping out of the ground that damaged lines or the truck. You had to put in low gear and keep an eye out for debris.

Blake got his first lesson in bribery from the boss. He would say you have to give the dog a bone so he would wag his tail. Go up to the operator and, fold up a twenty-dollar bill and hand him. This way, you were going to get in and out. What they would do is run it over, and at the end of the day, they had to cover it with a few inches of dirt. The residual waste from the landfill and the rain would run onto the roads and into the river.

They were destroying the Delaware River. Local Politicians, cops, and Judges were getting involved. There was talk about if you lived in Township, you didn't have to pay rubbish tax, the company paid for it. And around other townships cops were targeting trucks for debris and axel weight that creates Revenue.

There has always been an issue of the tons of solid waste is one of the biggest sources of environmental degradation in states and other countries. It contributes to pollution from off--surface runoff from rain. The chemical analysis of leachate is produced by the correspondence of the river or rivers.

There is an obsolete drainage system that doesn't contribute to the rivers and roads because they were built perhaps 100 years ago.

They are obsolete drainage systems in diameter that could not handle nature and mankind's waste. Another type of waste is methane gas.

Methane gas is emitted from a variety of anthropogenic (human-influenced) and natural sources. Anthropogenic emission sources include landfills, oil and natural gas systems, stationary and mobile combustion, wastewater treatment, and certain industrial processes.

Methane emissions pose a risk to the environment for various reasons one being it's about eighty times more powerful at warming the atmosphere than carbon dioxide over a twenty-year period.

# The Eighties

Global methane is the amount of methane in the atmosphere that has more than doubled since pre-industrial times, and the emissions are increasing faster now than they have since the 1980s. Methane also contributes to the formation of ground-level ozone, a gas that is harmful to humans, ecosystems and crops, according to an assessment.

High levels of methane can reduce the amount of oxygen breathed from the air. This results in mood changes, slurred speech, vision problems, memory loss, nausea, vomiting, and headaches. In severe cases, there may be changes in breathing and heart rate, balance problems, numbness, and unconsciousness.

There is also naturally occurring methane that is found below ground and under the sea-floor and is formed by both geological and biological processes. The largest reservoir of methane is under the seafloor. When it reaches the surface and the atmosphere, it is known as atmospheric methane.

The Earth's atmospheric methane concentration has increased by 150 % since the seventeen hundred, and it accounts for forty of the total radioactive forcing from all of the long-lived greenhouse gases. It has also been detected on other planets, including Mars, which has implications for astrological research.

The judge in the Township was a crook and making up his own law that you had to have your tri-axial down empty. There is nothing on it; its empty.

Government regulations determine the amount of weight by axels. The axial is made for the distribution of weight. If you didn't have it down empty, you got a ticket.

There was no doubt if they were charging by the yard companies so, companies would roll in with 90 to 100 thousand pounds. That was going on for years until the owners and the cops got wise, and that resulted in a new system of charging by the ton. That program is a huge Revenue and a failure. If it rains on the Refuse, it increases the weight. The Companies take a loss, and the consumer gets increased.

There were other places to go, one to Bethayers, South Philadelphia, Montgomery County, and Cinnaminson, NJ. Deptford NJ. And Mullica Hill, New Jersey. Before Once again, the boss got word that this guy was taking trash on his front lawn in the middle of the night in the winter time in New Jersey. It was frigid weather, with the load partially frozen. You had to dig it out by hand. It was a company that manufactured some type of vinyl fabric. An idea came out so the Rubbish owners would spray the sides with fuel so it doesn't freeze. That spot didn't last long Blake didn't go there anymore. Perhaps the Township stepped in? Who knows what the old man was thinking, dumping trash on his front lawn?

Even the street work customers were being billed for a larger can then what they were told. There was plenty of work involved in the city for everyone. There was a new Landfill opening up in Montgomery County. It used to be an old stone Quarry called Bethayers Quarry, right outside Northeast Philadelphia.

They took out so much stone they couldn't go deeper. The dumps were controlling haulers and that was taking out on the consumer. Not only that, the Government started classifying Refuse into different categories. At this time, a two-way radio was in-stalled in the truck. The money and the work were still rolling in.

Bethayers landfill was only supposed to take wood, brick, dirt, and block and or what is demolition. Word got out to other trash companies that were taking unwanted stuff in the beginning, perhaps mixed with paper or whatsoever? They were taking the money. The Trash men were getting away with it. Contamination occurs with trash being mixed with demolition. On a summer day, you could smell the stench from driving on the roads around the place.

When it rained, all that residual waste (Sewage) would rise and run into the creek, or they would pump it in there, most likely killed all the life. Blake was running up there for months and taking the loads to the quarry. Talk about luck! Some developers bought a mall on the outskirts of Philadelphia and joined with Montgomery County.

The owner had a carpet company, and he would keep a 30-yard cubic container next to the loading dock. There refuse was made up of card board and excess carpet material, complete with a 50-gallon liquid container of latex, and they were told to put it on bottom of the can.

The idea of taking it to Bethayers lasted for a while until they told Blake's boss to stop bringing the Latex in. A lot of the private haulers in the business were going there. It was buy the yard reasonable.

Blake also did a stop twice a month at a cemetery (John Doe's) off of broad at. They were burying so much trash in the commentary they ran out of room for graves. He was pulling some shabby old container. There were bags in them with loose flowers from grave sites, and was taking it to Bethayers and to South Philadelphia. He took it to South Philadelphia one time and pulled in and backed up to aa concrete pit and raised the rails, and flowers came out with crushed bones. He never said anything?

The Quarry had another incident; one of the Philadelphia Refuse company's brought in a load from a funeral parlor in North Philadelphia. The driver backs up and, opens the door, and unlatches it. He puts the rails up, and a casket comes out with a dead body coming out of it. Law Enforcement showed up. Blake does not know what happened thereafter.

The owners started to bring on more restrictions.

It wasn't long before Blake received his second and third lessons in Bribery from the owner; His second lesson was how to bribe a cop. Some went for it, and some didn't. It was a secret rhetoric that you said? Blake really cannot recall the words.

Blake had a habit of driving on bridges he didn't belong because of weight restrictions. Or should I say he was trying to take shortcuts? It caught up with him, and he got pulled over by a cop. In exchange for a traffic ticket, he bout tickets from the cop for The Philadelphia Police Motorcycle Show.

He was driving around for years and he bought a used car.

He was called into the shop one day, to the shop; the owner sent me over to his house be-cause there were neighborhood kids giving his daughter a hard time. The owner of the company sent Blake over to see what was going on. There were about eight or nine young adults standing across the street yelling or harassing her.

Blake went over and confronted the situation, and the next thing he knew, a fight broke out. He was cut with a broken soda bottle on his elbow, and it cut the tri-cep- tendon. He went to the hospital and had an operation, and lost 15 percent of his arm motion.

The owner told Blake he was going to report it to the insurance company that he fell off a dumpster. Blake had physical therapy a couple of times a week for a while. Blake stayed working or driving the roll-off and picking up dumpsters. Blake had to work for 2 years for nothing.

He had to pay a debt but there was plenty of work. The owner had 4 or 5 factories as steady customers, and some roofing, and street work, and a Seafood Restaurant. Per-haps a fifteen-yard container. You had to put the stop up three-quarters for axle weight.

That dumpster stunk, and perhaps often, when you went around a corner, the residual liquid would come flying out. It is what it was.

Another thing he had going on was a man who came over from Ireland. He brought crews of skilled workers and started rehabbing 4 story historical buildings and producing condos and rental properties with fireplaces and saunas in a section called Fair-mount that had four streets between Broad St. and 20th St. and Spring-garden and Fairmount Ave. It's a great location, blocks from Center city. The Courthouses, Libraries, Museums, and office buildings were only blocks away.

In fact, the area was becoming so popular politicians were getting involved. Green St was the focus of the whole neighborhood. The whole neighborhood had a drug problem or was taken over by drug dealers.

Perhaps some type of intelligence was involved? They managed to take down a few kingpins. After that, there was a mini Police station set up.

There was so much money and politics they closed down the neighborhood's Health center and, cleaned up the neighborhood, and made Condos. Lawyers, Judges, and Developers were investing in Historical 4-story houses for Tax breaks the President implemented to draw people to the city, colleges, and the arts and jobs.

Blake was going down there at night time swapping cans, dropping an empty, and picking up a full for the next day; little did they know the owner was giving him 16 cubic yards and being charged for twenty cubic yards. There was a man called Mick, who had a crew from Ireland to go in and demolition the houses and save the historical theme of items. He also had a crew of Masonry, Carpenters, Painters, and Electricians.

Old Mick, they say, came over from Ireland who had an Idea and a dream for the better of mankind and started working down from Eighteenth St. and was working east to 16th St. He was buying up the homes and making money; the area was hot. I was on call all the time, working days and nights and then finally it happened.

The boss asked Blake to go up to Montgomeryville and dump a load of trash behind some ski shop. He said Mick bought a Ski shop. I was laughing on that dark night when I pulled behind and opened the back door, and raised the rails, and out it came.

All the way up, he was saying to himself there is no way they were going to get away with this. This place (Township) was in Montgomeryville, Pennsylvania. I didn't say anything to my boss about it. Perhaps a day went by, and the boss got a phone call, and he was told to clean it up and nothing will become of it. Sure enough, Blake went back up and cleaned or reloaded the dumpster and took it back. Blake never heard a word about it again.

It wasn't long after that the doors started opening up. It was time for my third lesson on bribery. The boss came to me and said the Weigh masters were on the take in South Philadelphia. He said all the trash companies were paying them off. He told me what I had to do. Fold up a twenty-dollar bill and put it under the plastic card and hand it to them. Every time Blake gave a twenty-dollar bill to the weighmaster his boss gave Blake twenty. The Haulers were taking just about anything in there.

He started racing down with loads going in the morning and lining up with the other trash trucks. Anything after 40 hours was cash. This specific place was charging by the ton and tipping the scale; everyone was making money. The trash business was being run out of the house for years.

The owner had a master plan, and it was time to be implemented; he talked about how to beat the Landfills and have the other contractors and refuse companies coming to you. The master plan was the scrap yard that sat on a corner with a lot of land in the back.

The eldest son graduated out of high school and was soon learning the alloy business. The metallic substance composed of two or metals as a compound and solution for steel and metals. Of course, there are other metals with substances than copper, bronze, brass, and others for the benefit of mankind.

The owner of the company was a smart businessman and saved some money and went and talked to a man, Harry, who owned a small neighborhood scrap yard. The old guy made his money in the war. He knew he needed land to expand.

The property was massive, and the backyard went all the way down to the end of the block. And there were buildings on the other side of the block. In fact, there was an instrument company there, and they end up buying that property. It was time he was making his move on the scrap yard. His son ran the metal business with a helper who had worked for the previous owner.

They also hired a loader operator, who they took under their wing. There was a small concrete patio in the back of the shop where you couldn't see anything from the streets. A lot of loads were being brought in and dumped in the back to be recycled.

They installed a small truck scale alongside the building. There was also a gate to get in from another street. And then you could be right in the back of the place.

The trash business was bringing in a lot of money. They were transferring and working at a recycling station. The city was forcing him to use concrete for drainage purposes. The first thing they did was fortify the perimeter of the business putting up steel I beams and concrete huge walls.

There were carts that you put the Ferris or Non-Ferris metal in it, and it would be put on a small scale. They would buy for a price and re-sell it for a higher price. Ferris metals are such things as copper, brass, bronze, and other types. You had to separate and put in barrels to re-sell it. The yard had space for Light iron and steel. The scrap business was an old neighborhood place of business.

Everything was secretive. Blake couldn't tell you the exact size of the property at this time, but it had to be acres. It went down to just about to the other side of the next block with three little buildings on the end.

Also, loads of eighteen-wheelers. Every day, he was opening up the gates to get the truck out early. Do a route or list what had to be done? He was working at night time too. He remembers one time he was working at night and closing up the gates.

Blake left one night at the shop and was heading home, and it wasn't more than three blocks away when he was making a right turn when the 18 wheelers back wheels were running down the side of his car. He kept driving for some reason. He doesn't know what happened and the next day the car disappeared. Probably a week or two later, the check came from the insurance company. He was working all the time.

The owner hired a woman from College she had a BS degree in business and was working as a master manipulator with money. She didn't last long, perhaps a year, and then she married a millionaire next store who had a small instrument company. What a mess that was.

He had to hire in order to expand. He would tell me a story of a man who had a big manufacturing company, and all he did was hire Illegals on a work program? Just think you didn't have to pay taxes or Workman's compensation.

The owner also knew a woman who worked for Bell Tell she was transferring calls his way. It wasn't long but they bought a machine that grinded up wood and or skids to make mulch.

They started another offset business, but at the same time, it was related to demolition. The business started making a little money. Companies were bringing in trailer loads of skids to make mulch.

The owner got another tip and told Blake the Weigh Masters were fixing or tipping the scale in South Philadelphia.

The idea was told to him by an unknown source, you roll up a twenty-dollar bill and pass it under the account card. The Weigh Master was reducing the volume or weight size.

Blake was running down there three to four times a week and three or four times a day because every time they got twenty dollars, Blake got twenty dollars. The whole thing was going on for months and years. Blake caught the tail end of it.

The end was coming near; the boss said at the City Dump in Philadelphia, there was an investigation going on at the place. He was told from his boss we couldn't do it no more to stop.

Somehow, the cops or DA got wind that the Weigh masters were taking bribes, or it could have been a paper trail that started it. The largest Trash Bribery scandal. One judge tried to implement R.I.C.O., but the trash men got another Judge.

There were a dozen companies that got caught for bribery and taxes. The companies had good high profile Lawyers. These were family owned hard working people and the evidence was vague. One day, the boss tells Blake what we have to go to court.

He was told don't say anything at the primary hearing, and a month went by, and we were on our way to C.J.C., and all these people were packed in the court. The one Judge tried to say it was R.I.C.O., but the fix was in. They got another Judge.

He said we are going to sit in the back. They Judge was up there scratching his head and looking around at all these people lined up sitting down. We took a seat in the back of the courtroom, and Blake was told to keep his mouth shut. The judge said some things, and someone yelled out, what about Dick?

Dick was Blake's boss. No one said anything in court. Perhaps he was buying the one District Police Officers Bullet Proof Vests? Perhaps the methods he used were different and didn't draw attention. The boss never talked about anything or went into detail or a theory why they got away with it.

The D.A. picked out a name of a hat with everyone involved, and he was chosen to cooperate against the weigh masters. A lot of the companies got fined and some probation. A few of the big ones sold out for millions and retired

There was evidence with a lot of people involved. It was about a man who came up with an idea for money. And talk about that is was possibly handed down from their boss, by the way, who is living in a mansion in Florida.

The owner of the company never said anything. Perhaps he knew the cops and got the word? Perhaps he was or there was a rumor he was buying the district cops bulletproof vests? Perhaps the methods the owner used were different and didn't draw attention?

But no one talks about how much good Jon doe of America who no one wanted to do the job or care enough to do it. The grandfather of the Marrianni family started pulling a cart in 1880 to take away your waste. The hundreds of times when they paid all the churches in Philadelphia for a newspaper drive so students can earn money. These people knew more about Recycling paper than the Government or the Public in an early decade. The Business would soon be turned down to sons for generations. They would have 26 tractor trailers moving to The further step for recycling.

Paper, cardboard, and paper products exist in every facet of our lives, and they were one of the first families in the business to start recycling before it was mandatory.

There are many people who start their days with the help of paper products—the packaging of our favorite breakfast cereal contains paperboard, as does the carton of milk we use along with it. If some of that milk spills, you can clean it right up with a paper towel.

Our kids write, draw, take notes, build crafts, and read from textbooks every day in school using paper products. Adults do the same (often minus the crafts and textbooks) in our offices and workplaces.

The United States produces a lot of paper waste. The total

generation of paper and per board waste is in the millions of tons, according to the Environmental Protection Agency (EPA), which accounted for 23.1 percent of total municipal solid waste (MSW) generation that year.

We're able to recycle this much paper simply because of how recyclable paper is. While other materials, such as shrink-wrap plastic or used cooking oil (UCO), can only be reused two to three times, paper can be repurposed five to seven times before the fibers become too short and weak to be used again.

We have this family and other Trash men to thank for the overall rise in recycling over recent years. The paper industry has made great strides to educate consumers about the importance of recycling and to establish community recycling efforts to make the process even more straightforward.

Their efforts have paid off; nearly 80 percent of all paper mills in the United States used recycled paper to create new products.

America's landfills are getting filled with waste at an alarming rate. These landfills take up large areas of otherwise usable land and are the leading emitter of greenhouse gases that damage our atmosphere.

The environmental benefits of paper recycling cannot be understood. According to the EPA, recycling just one ton of paper can save 380 gallons of oil, 7,000 gallons of water, and enough energy to power the average American home for up to six months.

Paper recycling does conserves our natural resources. Recycling one ton of paper can save 17 trees from being torn down. Stanford

University recently recycled over 2,303 tons of paper, saving roughly 32,115 trees.

Paper recycling has benefits for businesses as well. Diverting paper from the landfill can dramatically reduce business waste costs, especially if your business churns through a lot of paper products. Companies with recycling initiatives can often receive tax credits from the Internal Revenue Service (IRS) and will have a better shot at engaging with eco-conscious consumers who only want to do business with sustainable organizations.

Before we get into the recycling process, it's important to note what type of paper products can be recycled at paper mills. These products include (but are not limited to.

Paper shredders are good for concealing personal information from any prying eyes, but they make recycling more difficult.

The small strips of shredded paper can easily become caught in the complex machinery of the recycling facility, damaging the machines or slowing down the entire process because the machines had to stop to rectify the stuck scraps.

It is uncommon for curbside recycling services to accept shredded paper, but some do, so be sure to check with your local facility before leaving any out.

The first step of paper recycling is collecting discarded paper to send to recycling facilities. We put paper into a separate recycling bin to keep it away from other waste products—contaminated paper, such as paper soiled with food, grease, or harmful chemicals, cannot be recycled and will be diverted to a landfill.

At the MRF, the paper is measured and sorted into separate categories, as certain paper products will be processed differently depending on the type. For instance, glossy magazine paper will be treated differently than a standard piece of printer paper, so they need to be sorted separately.

At the turn of the century, recovered paper is expected to supply 40% of all fiber used to make paper and paperboard products. There could be millions of cubic yards of landfill space. Recycling corrugated cardboard cuts the emissions of sulfur dioxide in half and uses about 25% less energy than making cardboard from virgin pulp.

After the paper has been sorted and checked for contaminants, it is baled together and sent to a paper mill, where the recycling process truly begins.

At the paper mill, paper is shredded down into small scraps. Large amounts of water and chemicals, like hydrogen peroxide, sodium hydroxide, and sodium silicate, are added to the shreds to further break down the paper into separate paper fibers. The result is a mushy concoction known as the pulp, the raw material that is used to make recycled paper. (This process is known as pulping.)

Larger contaminants, such as paperclips, staples, and tape, are screened for and removed from the pulp before it moves on to the next step.

The pulp, which is approximately 99 percent water to one percent fiber at this point, is then transferred to a paper machine.

Once the large contaminants have been removed, the pulp is put into a large floatation tank with more chemicals and air bubbles. The chemicals and air bubbles help remove dyes and inks from the pulp, enhancing the purity and whiteness of the pulp. Dyes can also be added during this process to create colored paper.

The pulp, which is approximately 99 percent water to one percent fiber at this point, is then transferred to a paper machine.

This is the final step in the paper recycling process. Once the pulp has been de-inked, it's passed through massive rollers to squeeze out excess water from the mixture. Once the moisture has been removed, the pulp is sent through heated rollers to form long rolls of continuous sheets of paper. From there, the rolls of paper are sent to various manufacturers to be produced into paper products.

There was talk that people would say the trash business was mafia-related. He never saw any such activity in Philadelphia. Most businesses were started by Old Relatives and grandfathers who came to America. Carting goes back to the eighteenth century. There was also people who got into it later on. Some people were saying the prices were too high. Ironic thing everything is too high in N.Y. I'm not saying it was or wasn't going on in New York, New Jersey, and Connecticut because they were having problems.

The Feds were moving in on the East Coast in the eighties. Some Crime families were supposedly controlling the businesses in New York, they also had property rights.

They were being accused of keeping potential competition from entering in the collection business. They were also being accused of paying bribes to public officials and unions. Prosecutors were seeking the forfeitures of 14 companies which were estimated at a worth of

100 million. Everyone was going to trial, and he couldn't tell what the end result was.

And perhaps the so-called Italian culture was targeted? The Italians and other American Cultures saw a need to haul waste because people couldn't live without it?

The largest Recycling Company in the world was forming and coming to the East coast. A story about a Dutch man who began hauling garbage at 1.25/ wagon in the north-west. His son and another man founded the company and started buying up smaller companies across the country. One of the decadents from the owner went public in the early seventies with 82 million dollars in revenue.

The company's network includes hundreds of transfer stations, and hundreds of active landfill sites, hundreds of recycling plants, and hundreds of Methane gas projects. In the seventies, the exciters of the company were cooking up the books by refusing to record expenses to write off the cost of the unsuccessful and abandoned landfill development projects.

Maybe establishing inflated prices and environmental reserves in connection with acquisitions with 82 million dollars. They also acquired another company.

An investigation was started in the seventies against these people. Failing to establish reserves for Taxes and other expenses; avoiding depreciation expenses for their trucks by unsupported by and inflating salvage values and extending their useful lives. Perhaps assigning values that had no value?

Failure in the decreases in the value of landfills as they were filled with trash used to eliminate maybe hundreds of millions of dollars in operating expenses. There were other rumors of offsetting against the sales or exchange assets. They were fined 30 million dollars.

A Waste company was forming out west, so he moved his headquarters. He would later get so big he was making his way to the East Coast.

It wasn't long when another of the owner's relatives came back in the picture. She wanted to start another Company recycling wood on the premises, and they bought a machine the size of a trailer that had an engine and grinder on it with a conveyer belt. It could make different sizes of wood and it's covered up.  The only problem was wood o skids have nails in them. Perhaps magnets were the answer Blake never told me. What he did say was any type of wood, concrete, asphalt, and or demolition could be recycled. Dick wasn't big enough to take on other trash companies, taking their stops. In fact, they would occasionally take his customers.

Some of these trash companies you just didn't mess with; they had more trucks or were in a better position, and a lot of the companies were family businesses I would refer to some things as the trash wars.

They had a policy if you didn't pay the driver, someone would come back and pulled up to your place and, open the backdoor, and dump it. In fact, the boss asked Blake to do it a couple of times. In fact, there was a restaurant trying to expand and clean up the back. He loaded it up with dirt and didn't pay. The owner told the driver to take it back in the heat of the night after closing and dump it on the sidewalk; it was done.

That soon changed; you had to pay before the can was delivered. The driver came to work one morning, and the front-end loader was firebombed. And one thing people couldn't understand with all those cameras all over the property was how no one was seen on camera in the yard. And all of a sudden, there was a new one. A few of his contain-ers disappeared. Perhaps the insurance covered it? He was at the point where he had to start buying new Dumpsters.

The gold mine was the backyard (Short dumping) on the property; it was a big hole, and he had to rebuild the loading dock so you could get a tractor-trailer in there so the trash could be transferred to a landfill. After he built the loading dock, he told the city inspector it was there when he bought the property.

The next move was to put a truck scale in, and sure enough, he started out with a small one that was on the side of the office and the metal business. Once that was done now he could take in small contractors dumping behind the building. Shorty and the loader operator were picking out what could be recycled, metal and a few items. There was a concrete pad behind it. From there, it would get transferred.

His son was learning more and more about metals and he was doing the buying and selling of the Non-Ferris and Ferris metals. The simple answer is that ferrous metals contain iron, and non-ferrous metals do not. The more in-depth answer is that ferrous metals and non-ferrous metals each have their own distinctive properties.

He had a helper who was working for the Company before they bought it an old guy from Southwest.

These properties determine the applications they are most suited for.

Non-ferrous metals have been used since the beginning of civilization. The discovery of copper in 5,000 BC marked the end of the Stone Age and the beginning of the Copper Age. The later invention of bronze, an alloy of copper and tin, started the Bronze Age.

The use of ferrous metals started in around 1,200 BC when iron production started to become commonplace. This ushered in the Iron Age.

Some common ferrous metals include alloy steel, carbon steel, cast iron, and wrought iron. These metals are prized for their tensile strength and durability. Carbon Steel – also known as structure steel – is a staple in the construction industry and is used in the tallest skyscrapers and longest bridges. Ferrous metals are also used in shipping containers, industrial piping, automobiles, railroad tracks, and many commercial and domestic tools.

Ferrous metals have a high carbon content, which generally makes them vulnerable to rust when exposed to moisture. There are two exceptions to this rule: wrought iron resists rust due to its purity, and stainless steel is protected from rust by the presence of chromium.

Most ferrous metals are magnetic, which makes them very useful for motor and electrical applications. The use of ferrous metals in your refrigerator door allows you to pin your shopping list on it with a magnet.

Non-ferrous metals include aluminum, copper, lead, zinc and tin, as well as precious metals like gold and silver. Their main advantage over ferrous materials is their malleability.

They also have no iron content, giving them a higher resistance to rust and corrosion and making them ideal for gutters, liquid pipes, roofing, and outdoor signs. Lastly, they are non-magnetic, which is important for many electronic and wiring applications.

Junior was a self-taught person with multiple talents in Business, Mechanics, and Metallurgy with knowledge, patience, and perseverance. He ran the business buying metals from neighborhood scrapers.

Little did he know, or perhaps he did know he saw an Empire. Blake had the vision potential, and the old man was smart and saw an empire.

Now contractors and other companies were coming in to dump. Blake was also going around and picking up cans and bring theming back to the yard more and more and dumping it right behind the metal shop on the patio and they would take out what could be recycled.

One term used is reducing volume and cutting out air space. It made sense if you could take in 80 yards and make it into 40 yards. There were only a handful of people working there. There was the owner, son, a Loader operator and a Laborer and Blake. The landfills stopped charging by the yard and started charging by the ton.

They would separate most of it and put it in a 40-yard container in the loading dock and, pack the rest of it with a backhoe, and run it up State Pennsylvania. He bought a Tri-Axle truck for this purpose with 75,000 Gross vehicle weight.  He would leave about eight or nine

O'clock from Philadelphia and arrive in the middle of the night up State. Pull in a dining area get something to eat and sleep in the truck and wake up early. There is always a line to get into the landfill; you wanted to be in it.

There was a time when his ex-wife asked me to come and sleep at her house. I told her I was alright. Blake would stay over until they opened. Race back and start all over. He was waking up early, and all day long, he was delivering and picking up dumpsters from factories, contractors and homeowners. 60 hours a week and a little more at times. Once the property was there, it was a gold mine.

A dumpster could cost anywhere between a couple hundred dollars to hundreds of dollars. The bigger the can, the more money they would charge. Blake went down center city to buildings to pick up containers. He wasn't thrilled about the rats. Every load had to have a tarp on it by hand. Once you picked up the can you looked in the mirror and saw these rats were jumping out. He wasn't going down there all the time.

And there was a rumor the guy next store was running a chop shop, and they were throwing parts over the fence. Blake knew he was hauling stolen parts to a larger Non-Ferris and Ferris Company who paid a higher price.

One day, Blake came to work, and the next store the place was crawling with F.B.I. Agents. The owner said the FBI was up the street on a telephone pole watching them. It was a truck chop shop, and even on occasions, they were throwing some stolen parts over the fence. Blake was running scrap metal to a larger company for money.

If there was dirt, concrete, and some wood, it would get dumped in the back of the place or yard. This way you didn't have to pay to dump. It was cash money, thousands and thousands of dollars in their pockets. The yard was expanding, and he had to make choices. He put the truck scale in and started pouring more concrete and building roofs. The next thing they bought was a concrete crusher, to make stone in different sizes.

And at this point in time, the owner started buying new containers, and he was driving down to New Jersey to get them. It was a manufacturing plant that made trash containers. It was also a nice ride up and back with the radio on.

They hired a retired cop, a sergeant to drive the tractor trailer to haul to the Landfill. They started out transferring the trash and recycles. They got rid of the Tri-Axle and got a tractor-trailer. Anything not recyclable at the time was sent to another Landfill. The back of the property went down to just about to end of the next bock. The hole was big for dirt and concrete.

The woman he hired didn't last too long, perhaps a year, and she married the guy next store who was a millionaire some years older than her. You could work them 10 hours and pay them for eight, or they were on a salary. They didn't want to make them citizens, and it was a means to keep them under control; it caused issues.

Plan B was taking in effect; concrete was being poured, and Steel beams were being erected around the property. And on one side of the property with metal roofs. The object is to take out as many recycled products as possible out. The more you recycled the less you went to the landfill. Demolition is different than household refuse. They bought a stone crusher.

It falls in another category because you are dealing with different substances. Demolition is wood, brick, stone, dirt, metal, and drywall.

On the ground, things were being segregated also: cardboard, books, drywall and Ferris, and non-Ferris metals. Any loads that came in with dirt or concrete were a double payment for the company.

The owner was taking in everything and charging buy the ton and paying by the yard. Recycling Substances or mass is a broad spectrum. For example, wood, brick, stone, asphalt, Non-Ferrous and Ferrous Metals, drywall, books, plastics, paper, cardboard, paints, oil, and dirt all can be recycled, and it goes deeper than that; they lined up 1 or 2 trucks at a time to dump on the concrete patio. It was a small crew. They used the guy in the metal shop and the front-end loader to sort.

The thing about recycled materials you got paid for it. There was a saying that the owner used in the business and that was (reducing volume and cutting out air space) in a container in various ways.

Philadelphia has a fascinating history of economic development that goes back centuries. Beginning with success and resulting in failure. It wouldn't be long before factories or manufactures were depleting and or moving their business down south. However, development was going on.

Blake started sword training; these techniques are often practiced many thousands of times before any degree of proficiency is obtained, which is why it is important to get proper instruction as practicing them solo without a sensei to instruct you can ingrain some seriously bad habits that will take years to un-train.

That he could execute a cut. Even the master considered himself a humble student, constantly striving for perfection and always felt clean, fast, and with better precision.

He would transfer the sword from his left hand to his right hand and then give it to Blake (symbolizing his intention is one of peace and learning). Some of the rules were designed to show that your intent in the training hall is to learn and to avoid threatening behavior or danger.

Others are amid on cultivating the correct mindset to build a solid foundation or openness. (Once you think you're so good at this, you have instantly stopped learning and, in fact, doing yourself a disservice).

To discard any elements is to miss out on cultivating the martial spirit of true mastery. Each style is different. Some start with the sword further back than others. Some finish it closer to the ground. None are wrong, just different approaches.

This is the most basic yet fundamental sword training cut. From (1) an overhead position, with the sword perfectly horizontal (check in the mirror to make sure), it is (2) cast out, much like casting a fishing rod by pulling with the left hand at the bottom, much like a lever until (3) it makes contact with the head or shoulder of the opponent and then (4) simply drops down to stop horizontally again. The action should be done without 'power allowing the blade to drop down.

A common mistake is to use too much force in the right hand, which is really only just guiding the blade. One way to minimize this is to practice the casting movement, holding the sword in the left hand only.

Much like the basic swing, the blade begins (1) facing out horizontally behind you and is (2) 'levered' by the left hand, arcing out with the (3) cut, making contact with the target and (4) cutting through the other side.

A vertical cut to the right side of the shoulder (and out through the left armpit) it (1) begins in the same position as the basic overhead cut and (2) then tilts slightly on a diagonal path as it is levered by the left hand.

With the feeling of casting a fishing line it (3) makes contact with the target as the arms are extended and the momentum.

4) carries through the target, finishing in a position slightly slower than horizontal, breaking with the elbows touching the body. Again, be sure not to power it with the right hand but let speed and the weight of the blade do all the work.

This is a very important point to remember whenever you do Japanese sword training - and you will notice the difference between an overly strong technique and a correct one by the sound it makes as it cuts through the air.

Contained within these seemingly archaic movements are many lethal techniques that, ideally at least, are based on tried and tested combat techniques.

(It has been argued that some schools are more 'pure' than others, with some supposedly being diluted during Japan's long period of domestic peace – though the frequency of duels between Samurai would suggest that truly ineffectual arts would not have been passed down through the generations, natural attrition would take care of that!).

In the case of the first few kata are often no more than drawing the sword, delivering a single strike, and then re-sheathing it. While on the one hand, these sword training methods were designed to be practical, training the swordsman by building fluid and economical movements deep into muscle memory with continual repetition.

That also served a greater purpose to develop single-minded, unwavering focus so that the warrior's mind would be clear, even in the face of death.

It may have been at this time when the owner came up with buying out one of Ville's front-end loading businesses.

It may have been 3 to 4 years later, and he started making money and, had a decent car apartment, and started to save money.

There were subcontractors lining up to take out refuse that couldn't be used or make money on it. Thousands of tons were coming in. A hundred and ten tons were being taken out a day.

Blake went to the owner and told him he wanted his own tractor to pull trash out of the yard. They wouldn't let me. Blake thinking after all the lying and cheating he did for the company, he would agree. The owner would not say how much he would have to pay per load. (Subcontracting). With your own tractor and trailer Blake thinks he could be making 300 to 400 hundred a day.

He was an atheist perhaps that had something to do with his business ethics. As long as he was cheating people and making money, he was in his glory.

Blake's mother called him and asked him how he was doing. She was glad he was working, and he offered to take her to The Art Museum to see the Vincent van Gogh exhibition. She agreed, and he bought the tickets for the next week. He was an eighteenth-century painter. He became one of the most famous figures in history.

He did hundreds of paintings that included portraits, landscapes and self-portraits. He drank heavily and neglected himself. He suffered from depression and poverty. On one occasion, he cut his Ear off, but it was fixed.

Van Gogh was commercially unsuccessful during his lifetime, and to some, he was considered a madman, perhaps because he cut his left ear off. He became famous after his suicide and was seen also as a misunderstood genius. I made the arrangements, and that weekend, I also went for a country drive up 232 for a day.

A place called New Hope, with antique shops and outdoor cafés. You park your car at the end and stroll around. It was a small town that sits on the Delaware River between New Jersey.

Perhaps years went by, and somehow, he got in contact with an old friend from California, a movie star. He flew over from California. And the three of us had a meeting. He wanted The Master to open up a school in Washington D.C., And they wanted Blake to go and be the instructor. They wanted me to pack up and go. The Master had warned

Blake that he foresaw if he didn't go with him, he would go back to his old ways or a life with no direction.

He told him he would think about it. Part of Blake knew what he said was going to come true. He spent another 6 months working or giving him a hand with his English.

A week went by, and Blake called his mother to take her to the Vincent Van Gogh exhibition. He drove up to her house and picked her up and took her to The Art Museum. Parked the car and entered, His styles and works of portraits, flowers, orchards, and wheat fields were genius. We found the Sunflower portrait in August of 1889 fascinating.

The whole thing was an elating experience, the exhibit and spending time with his mother. They talked on the way home and had a nice day.

Monday was here, and it was time to go back to work. Blake had a bad attitude toward these sneaky people. He wanted so bad to go in the trucking business and they wouldn't do it. I got the sense it was bullshit them telling me they would make me Vice President, but they wanted him driving a trunk. You have to understand the situation at the time. The owner had two sons who were working there, to. Dick's sister thought he was a selfish person in fact it was said before she went to her deathbed.

The eldest son was a brilliant, straight, hands-on guy. His brother was a misfit or perhaps a smart fox?

His younger brother was always getting thrown out of school, and before Blake knew it he was driving him to another school in the trash track. After that he got thrown out of Valley Forge Military Academy.

The owner's sister worked in the office for a while, and what she was doing and how much she was being paid, she quit.

And the owner's daughter started back working in the office and was changing policy now. She insisted on time and a half and no more cash. Just losing thousands of dollars on the scam and now the cash was a pay cut. They wanted to cut his cash off, and pay time and a half.

At or getting near the end, Blake was making close to thirty thousand dollars a year until the bribery scam was uncovered and cash after 40 hours. In fact, he was probably taking home in his pocket 500.00 dollars a week. That was a lot of money in 1984 and 1985.

He starts running numbers in his head: 9x40 = 360.00 dollars a week, and can I say 10 or fifteen hours' overtime 13.50x10= 190.00 dollars. Perhaps a pay cut? The owner's plans included buying more trucks. He also started buying new containers.

That was a nice ride going down South Jersey to a manufacturing company that made different-sized containers. In most cases, he started buying 20-yard containers. They were good for dirt, concrete, cleanouts, shrubbery, and manufacturing companies.

The economy was good in the eighties that operated on the basis of supply-side eco-nomics—the theory that advocates lower tax rates so people can keep more of their income. Proponents argue that supply-side economics results in more savings, investment, production, and, ultimately, greater economic growth. It all was real in the early eighties.

In the 1980s, Philadelphia mob boss Nicky Scarfo presided over one of the deadliest periods in Mafia history and ordered the murders of nearly 30 members of his own organization. Nicodemo Scarfo was known as "Little Nicky" for his 5-foot-5-inch stature. But he more than made up for it with his violent temper. Scarfo was so ruthless that he was once said to have exclaimed, "I love this. I love it," with joyous excitement while watching his soldiers tie up the body of an associate he'd ordered killed for allegedly insulting him.

It soon became too much for his captains, who feared his unpredictability and slowly began informing on the family. The final blow came when his own nephew, Phil, who'd been at his side for a quarter-century, turned on him to avoid a 45-year prison sentence in 1988.

And when Nicky Scarfo was sentenced to 55 years in 1989, he became the first mob boss in American history to have been personally convicted of murder — and joined the infamous ranks of bosses whose personal ruthlessness brought an ignominious end to their entire organization.

In fact, Blake gave the Master his answer and said goodbye. Somehow and some way Blake ran into an old friend who he had met and knew about since he was fifteen years of age. He wanted to split a two-bedroom apartment. He introduced him to the night-life.

He was in his last year of college, getting a degree in Accounting. He was also working part-time for a car dealership. The degree he said does not pay good unless he was a Certified Public Account or what is also known as the C.P.A. test.

He was fortunate too; his parents were upper middle-class people who lived outside the city in a single-family home sitting on a nice property.

We would go out clubbing or going to nightclubs to meet woman. I wasn't a drinker at the time. We were going out to the mainline or South St to the night clubs.

One of his favorite places was South Street that was known for multi Garment stores, Restaurants, Artists, and entertainment of all sorts. It's attached to an eight block stretch with a few adjoin streets we would go down and stroll around. Get something fine to eat and talk to or dance with some ladies.

At this time a, Trash Too Steam was becoming more popular and lucrative. The method of incineration to convert Municipal Solid Waste (MSW) is a relativity old method of WtE generation. In other words, burn the waste to boil water, which powers a steam generator that generates electricity and heat. Furthermore, the owners of Landfills started charging by the ton in fact there were a few who didn't that were left.

They also bought a Luger. A Luger truck was good for small containers, specifically for ten-yarders or an eight-yard container. They asked Blake to give a driver a road test, he did and passed him. Sometime later the guy got into an accident, and they fired him. They came and said to Blake and said I thought you said he could drive. He drove fine on the road test.

Blake moved off of Rising Sun Ave in Philadelphia, Pa. he got an apartment and was still hauling trash. She was a schoolteacher. he pulled up at a red light and struck a conversation with her and started dating.

At this time, he was driving a Red 914 Porsche, A Volkswagen motor in the back. Targa top. He would take her on drives to New Hope and browse. We dated for some time and had a child together a little girl, she died in the hospital. The relationship went downhill.

It didn't matter at this point the yard was growing, trucks and dumpsters with heavy equipment was being bought. Refuse is an all year around business, six days a week. Days and weeks, and months and years were going by. Blake felt as though he was deliberately being held back. The trash was coming in perhaps 200 tons a day. Who knows what the hauler was getting could have been hundreds of dollars being taking out, four or five loads a day.

It depends what company he subcontracted to. The money was there and Blake could afford to save. He lived in a nice area (Fox Chase) on the outskirts of the city; a two-bedroom apartment was 400.00 dollars a month. Car insurance was cheap especially if you had a clean driving record. And gas was perhaps less than a dollar a gallon and it helped.

There was an old saying that if you made money in one week to cover your rent, you could get ahead, and he was doing that. There is a lot of truth to that. It was happening, but the big money started rolling in a little at a time.

There were family members there, and their idea was to keep him driving for twenty or so years. He was one of the best Roll-Off drivers in the city and could pick up anything. The yard was an enormous size he said it before and they focused on that. Blake felt betrayed and cheated in a code of honor, keeping his mouth shut.

His reasoning was he still wanted his own tractor, their paying Blake 9.00 dollars an hour, and he said to himself when he knew he could be making hundreds a day, and perhaps thousands. It's more responsibility, starting out with a tractor and then a trailer When he was watching a 100 tons a day were being Subcontracted out, and learning minor and some big repairs and problems that can come with it. Sure, why couldn't he start out with these people after all they were supposedly family? GOD Forgive Me for Lying and cheating for them. What does a man do for money to lose his soul?

Blake would have needed a place to park the truck and why not their yard? They owned just about a whole block. They could have hired a driver? He was accumulating knowledge of the Trash business and hauling. He didn't know anything about freight hauling. Blake felt being used and conspired against by the kids.

He started a little bit from not feeling and or not being right mentally and physically. One night, he was drinking and looking for some cocaine late at night.

Not far from the shop after work. He headed down 2nd St and, made a right on a one-way street and side-swiped a car; the neighbors came running out and grabbed him. Before he knew it, he was downtown in what is called the Roundhouse. He enters the jail and his bosses his Ex-wife's brother, is working there as a cop for many years.

What are you doing here, he said? A car was hit. Shut your mouth, and you will be put in a cell. They shifted him around to a couple of different cells; everything is cement, and it's a dirty place. Hours went by, and he tried to get some sleep. It was early in the morning when Jack came to the cell and said just walk out. The fix was put in. His boss did not say much, but he knew he was having problems. Five years, he did not pick up a drink, and he started again.

The other factor when hauling trash, it takes a special trailer for it. There are two kinds at the time was a Packer and a Walkout.

They decided to teach Blake how to drive a tractor-trailer. The Walkout was the most common one. The top of the trailer was open and that was how it was loaded. The sys-tem was run by a hydraulic pump and lines that moved the floor back and forth.

Roll on the scale and pull up out of the way, and un-tarp before you got to the spot where it was going and then go to the spot. Follow the operator signs and pull back, and open the door.

You had two hook up two lines from the trailer and engage the pump (Power Take Off). That would activate the floor that would move or slide back and forth to move the trash out while it rolled forward. They taught him eventually how to drive a tractor-trailer. He was about to go from a class B to a class A license.

The maximum gross weight of any combination is 80,000 lbs. These limits are subject to the registered gross weight of the vehicle, requirements regarding axle weight and requirements regarding wheel load. Vehicles are also subject to any weight restrictions applied to particular roads or bridges.

It was at this time the Government was imposing regulations on waste on businesses and households. The separation of some household items such as cardboard and plastics, were being implemented.

Incinerators were still being built a room filled with garbage, a claw reaches down and grabs 4 tons of trash and drops into a shaft into an oiler that's hotter than 1,500 degrees Fahrenheit. The process continues 24 hours a day, seven days a week. In some countries it reduces the trash sent to landfills. Methane is generated from organic waste in landfills. In the short term methane is about 70 times more potent than carbon dioxide.

Heat is transferred into steam that spins turbines to generate electricity like conventional power plants. Garbage supplies much of heating during cold months for millions of residents.

Energy from trash equals the heating demand of 1.25 million apartments and 700,000 homes. Where is your electricity going in your area? The centralized district heating warms many buildings.

Along with heat and electricity, some countries produce methane biogas from 100,000 tons of organic waste. This biogas can run city buses as well as trucks and taxis. Using Methane for fuel is like a time bomb (Huge Explosion) when impacted on the tank from a collision?

However, some say garbage fueled power plants are not a clean energy source. In fact, some opponents claim these power plants are a "false solution" that green wash-es a dirty incineration. The process of burning trash is inherently polluting. You can put state-of-the-art pollution controls on an incinerator in the same way that you can a coal plant but that doesn't make the air cleaner. After five years, Blake quit his job at the Recycling Center.

Blake got into contact with a guy he grew up with and asked him if he wanted to go partners on a four-story historical house. It was almost like a race for this section with some investors. President Bush gave a tax credit on Historical property.

Blake left his job for a four-by-four-block radius for extravagant housing or condominiums. It was right off of Spring Garden, which was only 5 blocks to City Hall. Anyway, between Broad and 20th St and between Fairmont to Spring Garden Avenue. Developers were coming in. The Philadelphia Community College was right on Spring Garden St., which was right down the street. This was all elite work done with fireplaces and, in some cases, saunas. There were some called shells. Ideas take passion, perseverance, and determination, and money in this case.

The plans of the building were being made into three apartments, two one-bedrooms and One bi-level two-bedroom, with a deck. He ended up going partners on a house for fifteen thousand dollars on Mt. Vernon St. One block below, Mick was building for some time and five blocks long. The Art Museum.

The properties were getting slim to buy. They were competing or trying too with builders. Developers and a Judge or too who were twice their age and they had money backing them up.

Furthermore, they didn't have all the figures about construction cost. Blake had twelve thousand cash and Hat had the same. They hired an architect. Complete with Fireplaces and Saunas were in the plans. Blake knew of a man he grew up with who when it came to construction he was very knowledgeable and talented with his hands. His father was a Master builder.

They had to demolish the inside of the building and then frame it out. By then there was 35,000 dollars into it. A 100 more thousand was needed to finish it they were was told. Blake made a phone call to a guy who owned a Trash Company and wanted to talk to him about lending him the money. Blake was not in his right frame of mind. If the property was finished most likely it would have been worth a quarter of a million dollars at the time. Top of the line. Blake sold out.

His old boss came down with his son and suggested coming back to hauling trash and finishing it.

His partner had a job. It was soon after that one of the builders came by and told me at this point, I should finish one apartment at a time. It was the way to go. We could not continue on so he backed out and took on another partner.

Philadelphia has a fascinating history of economic development that goes back centuries It had everything The Industrial Revolution, Cars, Planes, trains, skyscrapers, bridges, roads, and garments, and to all manufacturing with success and resulting in failure. In the early nineteenth century

A neighbor who Blake grew up with received a large sum of money and had a Cocaine and alcohol problem. He had a lot of problems at an early age. His older brother died from pills and alcohol.

Years of driving the trash truck, Blake noticed all types of people and been in every neighborhood in the city. Blake was out of work, and he got a phone call from Hollywood. Yes, that's his name.

Anyway, he called Blake and asked him if he could get him seven grams of Cocaine or a quarter ounce. He had to drive to a section in Philadelphia, Pa., they called little Porto Rico. 5th Street stretched for blocks in and around in directions with drug dealers. Fifth and Indiana is where he met a man on a corner. The transaction was made it was said he made a hundred dollars a trip. At this time, Cocaine was being made into crack by cooking it with one-third of Baking Soda and other substances and then smoking. They called it Freebasing. In the early 1980s, a highly addictive drug called "crack" hit city streets. Crack—cocaine sold in a rock form instead of a powder—was also a pharmacologically different than powder cocaine but delivered the drug's high to the brain faster and more intensely than cocaine taken alone or heroin.

He does not recall but he thinks Regan was the President a great Republican who cared about America. Reagan implemented "Reaganomics", which involved economic deregulation and cuts in both taxes and government spending during a period of stagflation. He escalated an arms race and transitioned Cold War policy away from détente with the Soviet Union. Reagan also ordered the invasion of Grenada in 1983. Additionally, he survived an assassination attempt, fought public-sector labor unions, expanded the war on drugs, and was fast to respond to the AIDS epidemic in the United States, which began early in his presidency. In the 1984 presidential election, he defeated former Vice President Walter Mondale in another landslide victory. Foreign affairs dominated Reagan's second term, including the 1986 bombing of Libya, the Iran–Iraq War, the secret and illegal sale of arms to Iran to fund the Contras, and a more conciliatory approach in talks with Soviet leader Mikhail Gorbachev that culminated in the Intermediate-Range Nuclear Forces Treaty.

Furthermore, the President also realized The drug epidemic in America. The Cartel's main delivery State was Florida. It was being brought in by Speed boasts, fishing, and airplane drops. Florida was a source of distribution to all of America. The amount of violence and deaths was rising from drugs. He set up a task force, and within years, they got hundreds of money and drugs. They soon realized the problems were worse and set up four more task forces. Later on the Cartels soon realized they needed a better port of entry. They targeted Texas, starting digging tunnels and paying people to cross the border. And the old saying, Planes, trains and, automobiles, and submarines.

"Once you try crack, it is said, you're always 'chasing the ghost'—the high that you get the first time is so intense that you can never achieve it again, but the desire to do so is strong enough that you keep pursuing it.

"Cocaine had long been a rich person's drug, but this changed as drug entrepreneurs transported cocaine along with heroin from the Caribbean, Colombia. and Latin America into the United States. "Over time rival Colombian cartels produced too much cocaine, and oversupply and competition drove down the price in the American market." Affordable "across the class structure," cocaine "became part of American recreational life more than any other illegal drug except for marijuana, reaching a high point in 1980 when nearly 20 percent of eighteen-to-twenty-five-year-olds reported that they had tried cocaine in the previous year." Occasional recreational snorting of cocaine was addictive. It was also the largest illegal business in America, with billions of dollars.

This wasn't the case with freebasing, "a volatile process of mixing cocaine with another chemical, usually highly flammable ether Baking Soda, heating it, and then reducing the residue to a crystallized alkaline form," which, when smoked with a water pipe, "produced . . . a powerful and nearly instantaneous high" if the user didn't first go up in flames. Enterprising dealers soon discovered a process to "produce a prepackaged form of freebase that delivered the punch without the problem of self-immolation and did so at a fraction of the cost of powdered cocaine." They cooked a mixture of cocaine, baking soda, and water.

Boiling off the water left "a hard rock-like substance called crack from the sound that it made when heated." Sold in vials, crack "rocks" could be smoked, with the fumes delivered rapidly into the bloodstream.

Crack was devastatingly addictive. And the behavior of crack addicts was volatile, desperate, and often violent. The crack phenomenon destroyed lives, disrupted families, and undercut traditional values along with putting the country in ruins. Addicts turned to crime, often stealing from their own kin, to find the money to "chase the ghost."

From the early 1980s through the 1990s, urban America experienced soaring rates of addiction and crime to this powerfully addictive drug. 4 murders a day in California.

The hardest-hit cities were in the Northeast and Mid-Atlantic, specifically the tinder-box areas of concentrated poverty and high unemployment, with easily available guns.

Crack cocaine reached epidemic proportions in Philadelphia between 1983 and further on, a period that saw some 500 dealers indicted by federal, state, and local authorities. In one notorious example, the organization headed by Antonia Rivera, a North Philadelphia drug kingpin, grossed $3.5 million (netting a $1 million profit) within a twelve-month period, employing youths aged fifteen to seventeen to sell $5 vials of crack. Police Commissioner Willie L. Williams said that "dozens and dozens" of drug blocks existed throughout the city.

In March, some people presided over the demolition of a block of abandoned row houses in North Philadelphia's "Badlands" that were havens for heroin junkies and crack pipers. There was a stronghold.

The Badlands (Kensington Philadelphia) was the "nerve center" of Philadelphia narcotics trafficking. "The heart of the Badlands is square-miles an outdoor bazaar set in a harrowing stretch of blown-out row houses and graffiti-splashed buildings," that "runs, roughly, from Front Street to Germantown Avenue and from Huntington Street to Allegheny Avenue." The federal Drug Enforcement Agency (DEA) estimated that drug dealing there (cocaine, crack cocaine, and heroin) yielded a profit of at least $450 mil-lion.

Overseeing this underground economy were "150 to 200 known drug possess of 10 to 50 people," which controlled approximately 70 percent of the city's drug market; about half of the trade involved suburban buyers.

The Government classified Crack when it was made with other ingredients. Various ways were being formed and sold cheaply for two dollars. It was being cut, come back, alcohol and perfume. I'm sure there are more types of additives. Adding other chemicals or substances, you get more volume out of the product. At one time, the guidelines in the Judicial system were more severe for selling it, but not anymore, a slap on the wrist. Stove-top burners were being used, and then it was figured out how to do it with Microwaves.

Blake was going down there for Hollywood a couple of times a week, inflating the price and tapping the bags. The powder Cocaine was sniffed by a straw or bill and could be injected.

And going over to another guy's house in the neighborhood to sell, he would take a little, and they would shoot pool and have some beers. And also go down the basement. There was a radio, ping pong table, Dartboard and Bar and, radio, and homemade wine. And a wood stove for heat. They had a canopy of grapes growing in the backyard that led to the Garage and that always had a case of beer in it.

Blake knew some roofers from the trash business who did Cocaine he got it touched with a few and they were satisfied with the product, perhaps a gram for seventy dollars, It was said he was doing that for some months running down to Little Puerto Rico for Cocaine.

Blake didn't see his old neighbor for years. He grew up with his family as a child. His brother got married some years ago. He bought a fixer-upper house that was located on a creek. The houses on the street would flood from rain storms.

His house was mainly built on the second floor, so water damage didn't occur. He didn't know at the time why the Township would deal with the flooding problems. The creek, or small river, after years of erosion, expanded wider towards the houses.

It was a small community that was peaceful. More or less, it was a blue-collar working neighborhood. Most people knew one another.

There were various ways to combat the problem: dirt, stone barricades, and trees being planted to rebuild and restore it There was the creek that, when it rained it flooded out one side of the houses. On the other side of the street and then a row of houses spread out in perhaps 3 acres. It was a small development. The talk started, and the township wanted to buy everyone out and make it a natural habitat.

Some people sold out, and others wouldn't. It became a dispute with other neighbors who wanted to stay. The Government has failed Americans and neglected the creeks and small rivers because they never addressed the erosion problem. In some cases, they have gotten so wide that there is little or no water in some spots until it rains. Fish are unable to have places of habitats.

The township did buy some houses and would leave them to dilapidation and or just let them sit there without tearing them down. The whole idea was to make a natural habitat or park?

Blake occasionally stopped by and said high. At this time, he was married and had two kids. Often talked about current issues and sometimes, some people we knew would come up and get together and shot darts and drink beer.

The next day when he awoke and did some things, he went Downtown to a restaurant bar and met a woman. She was like a glow-in-the-dark. She wore a skirt, blouse and a coat. He asked her if he could buy her a drink. Of Course, she said. And we started talking. She would talk in spontaneous actions. By the way, my name is Blake and yours? Lisa, nice to meet you!

With her expressions is what enriched him with desire and also her mind had knowledge of the Sciences, Arts, Music and economic issues. Right now the river was beside us and the waves were breath taking and also in harmony. He was sitting there thinking what was going to become of this relationship that started to reveal things about one another, having an overflowing that had a richness about her exclusive bounds and wishes that were reasonable and desires. She was the type of woman when you observed her she had the same balance as two intellects with perspective. She was also the type of woman who would hold you captive with the pleasantness in her eyes, she talked for hours, and he listened too.

She had an inspiration, purpose, and enthusiasm to live, and it was catching. She was used to having an order or schedule that gave her an inherit sense of time. Blake offered to cook some food over my place for some French Bread pizza.

She agreed and followed me to my place. We headed for the kitchen and gathered all the ingredients together I got the sausage, the bread, and pizza sauce.

I asked her to chop up; 4 ounces of mozzarella cheese shredded

2 ounces of Colby cheese shredded

2 ounces of parmesan cheese shredded

He preheated the oven to 350 F and placed the sausage in a medium skillet. And then cooked it over a medium-high heat and I stirred frequently until brown and crumbly for about eight minutes and then drained well.

He also cut the loaf of bread on a board, in a half lengthwise, then in half horizontally, making four pieces from the loaf of bread. I than placed the pieces cut side up on a baking sheet.

Blake told her he was getting a bottle of wine better than 90% of all others. What made it rare was the balance of production; Barbeito Madaira vintage that he had put aside for an occasion. He poured her a glass of wine. She than asked me if she could make Carrot Cupcakes for desert. I told her to go ahead all the ingredients are here.

Blake divided the sausage, onion, bell pepper rings, mozzarella, and the Colby and parmesan evenly over the top of each piece. I placed it in the oven for about ten minutes so the edges would brown or until done. Blake set the table to sit down and eat and called her name and said time to eat, and he went to the oven and served her and myself. they sat across from each other, and I told her I hope you like it. I got up from the table and topped her wine glass off, she smiled. Sat down and finished my meal. There were no words spoken at the table. When I finished, I got up and rinsed my table ware and put in the dishwasher. I left her alone to eat.

He turned the oven off. She came out and rinsed her plate off and put it in the dishwasher. Let me do it she said. She sprayed one 12-cup muffin with nonstick cooking spray.

She combined all the ingredients and filled each muffin cup three quarters full with batter. Blake was having a nice time and the glow in her face expressed the same thing. The pan was put in the oven for baking perhaps 20 minutes. Meanwhile, she was making the glaze.

He went to the bookshelf and picked out a book and sat down on his chair and started to finish or read where he left off. She came out from the kitchen with a platter of some cupcakes. Thank you, I'll take two of them. What is the book about, she said?

Various issues about History: we can't solve the world's problems, it's too trenched with Corruption and Evil. Corruption by Old Age, Treachery, Tyranny, Clash of Cultures, and Conquest. I am going to close my eyes and feel free to do whatever you would like. That's the last thing he remembered, he fell asleep on the chair.

Blake was awoken by a tap on his arm and couldn't believe it she made breakfast for him. He thought he was dreaming. She made two eggs sunny side up, home fries and asparagus, wheat toast, and orange juice and milk. O' my goodness, he said to himself, she had slept in his room.

He thought it was explainable; it was actually one of my favorite meals. She served me and handed me a piece of paper with her name and phone number, and said call me. It dawned on me when I met her I didn't even ask her name?

He cleared up everything and washed the dishes and went into the bathroom brushed his teeth and took a shower, and got dressed and that's when he got a phone call. He was an associate growing up. He had just got out of the Marines with Top clearance and asked Blake if he wanted to be one of his drivers at night. They talked, and he said no he was not available tonight. As soon as he hung up he got another phone call from Hollywood and asked him to get him a quarter ounce seven grams of cocaine.  He never asked him what he was doing with it, snorting, shooting, or cooking it.

Hollywood had a lot of problems even as a child he tried to blow up the Gas station early on in his life. He lost his brother from alcohol and pills, and right before he got in touch with him, he shot himself in the head with a gun, but survived.

And then he got hit by a bus and was thrown in the air, and landed on the sidewalk. Perhaps he was suicidal?

He was on his way to his house so when he arrived, he parked out front and walked around the back of the house. Blake knocks on the basement window only because he lived down there.

He came outside and handed the money over and said I'll see you soon. Blake left and went on his route down Huntingdon pike through Rockledge to church road down to Second Street to Rising Sun Avenue to second street. Once you left the township all the way down were unfriendly people.

The city at the time was turning from bad to worse. Geographic areas and or districts is majority crime-ridden. Certain neighborhoods were worse than others. Plagued with drugs, guns and or crime. Once arriving close he would go down to Lehigh Ave. Every other street in Philadelphia is a one way. Come up 5th street and park on the corner of fifth and Indiana.

He got out and walked up and made the transaction and started his car up and went on his way. Occasionally driving different routes back to his house He took his share and delivered it to Hollywood. A little over an hour trip up and back.

On this day, Blake decided to go to Center City, or what is known as South Street, and eat at Walt's Crabs on Second street and South. It delicious and left and on his way he thought about calling Lucy for dinner. I had a good she enjoyed my cooking and was going to offer it to her tonight. I parked and, went inside, and sat down. This a friendly, polite place with good food. How can I help you Sir?

I'll have a bowl of Mussels in garlic sauce with bread and a glass of bear. And also the Crab Saffron risotto: with your quality Arborio rice. I'll take the mussels first. One of my favorite spots to eat, the food was well-balanced with seasonings.

Texture is always good with refreshments. The Mussels just came out, and are very delicious. Pardon me for finishing up my meal. How was everything Sir? Just fine, thank you, and I'll take my check, please. He felt good and walked to his car and decided to go home and relax.

It was a nice sunny day with clouds all around and about. His apartment was in an area that's called Five Points in northeast Philadelphia.

About a half hour drive depending on traffic? Arriving home and going inside and heading to the kitchen to make a cup of tea with honey and sat on the chair and picked up a book.

He was reading a certain book for some time that has knowledge amassed with understanding, and comprehension of the truth and facts that are tested and, coordinated, and systematized, especially calling the wide generalization of humans for a couple of hours and then decided to go take a nap in his bedroom.

He was awoken by a phone call a few hours later by Frank needing a driver for tonight; what's entail is what was asked. When the suns go down, I'll be working and you will get a phone call to meet me at a Garment factory in North Philadelphia. And then, I'll set the alarm off and get dispatched to the locations. I have all the keys too. You have to be there to load up the car. It could be anything Suites and fine made sweaters.

When my shift ends we go to a bar in Olney and take everything out and spread it on the pool table and in and around and sell it. Frank also stated he had keys to warehouses or small distributors of cigarette distributors. They are expensive products and the return is good. Call me later frank and I'll let you know?

The whole thing was easy money; however, Blake thought it's a means to an end. In other words, it would be a matter of time before management would discover that thousands of dollars of products would be missing. The numbers would not lie in inventory. So therefore he said no.

Blake hoped in the shower and shaved and dressed casual and decided to go to The Billiard hall. On the drive the thought of the Garment industry crossed his mind that started in the late eighteenth century. The manufacturer of ready-to-wear clothing be-came industries. Early in the nineteenth-century clothing was still being produced by women in their households or custom-made for Tailors and seamstresses. At one time 90% of clothing was being made for all of America. They were making clothing for The Armed forces and other companies, blue collar outfits.

Since WWII, the once vigorous garment industry has dwindled in the sixties and seventies. Many companies sold off and started to close, leaving tens of thousands out of work. How do you compete with companies and foreign industry workers working for two dollars a day, housing, and rice?

Pulling up in front of the billiard hall, Blake went in. He grabs the pool stick and walked in. And who did run into Earl the Pearl? That was his nickname. He was always a worthy pool player or competition. They were from different neighborhoods but ran into one another at an early age.

Blake rented a table for an hour and played 8 ball, Rotation and 9 ball, and played a few games. There was soda, and a snack machine took his time buying a pack of crackers? It was a recreational hobby. Pretty much the hour was used up, so it was decided to head back to the Apartment. It was a good time, always enjoying the hobby and reminiscing.

Went in and grabbed a soft drink, and sat down sat down. Blake cleaned up the bath-room and vacuumed the rugs and put away the dishes and watered the plants. He also started thinking about what Frank was doing hitting these factories out of control. The crack is what was driving him and that causes stupidity.

He thought it better if he didn't want to get involved for the simple reason it wouldn't be long. It just so happened the end was getting near anyway it wasn't too much long-er for the simple reason of inventory producing a count and then verified and then a lower count was discovered by owners.

It was the same concept at the cigarette vending company. Boxes of cartoons start coming up short, so the wheels of the mind start turning.

Security Company filed charges but had no evidence so he got fired. The Crack Pandemic was his downfall at the time in the early eighties it was cheap, and tons were flooded on the streets of Philadelphia and crossing the country. Crime rose to an all time.

For two dollars, you could buy some in a small plastic vile, corners were set up all over and or have been, and it was another product being put on the streets besides Heroin and Powdered Cocaine. The three combinations of these substances is a far cry of history. So he left it alone.

It was a systematic study of the Arts and Sciences that drew Blake to the Art Dist. The musicians and Artists come out the First Friday of the month to show and promote their skills. The crowds are enormous, with diversity. He headed down.

And a sweetness with calmness by the winds of nature. He began walking around, looking at all the different types of handcrafted, Paintings and Musicians It was a four-block radius by four blocks. Blake decided to go down at 2nd and Arch to see The Guitar player and violinist. As he stood there listing for a second and there she was approaching the scene with two of her friends.

She was captivating with mysteriousness about her, perhaps from human knowledge fitted to inspire. Perhaps, in something related to the intellect or understanding of the mind?

Blake gazed at her with a smile, and at that point, she did the same thing. Therefore, he walked over and started a conversation. The Violin is my favorite instrument he said. me too, I enjoy the Arts and Music. I'm sorry, my name is Blake, and yours? Lisa. Please to meet you. We talked, listening to the violinist and gaiter player.

Would you like to go for a drink? Why not?

She told her girlfriends she was going for a drink and they just smiled and waved goodbye. While walking to the bar restaurant, he couldn't stop thinking about the wonderful fragrance in the air she admitted. We arrived at the Pub. What are you having, Lisa? I'll have a dry martini. A bartender can we have two dry martinis?

"Yes, Sir, coming right up.

"It's lovely out, Lisa. Yes, it is.

Who is one of your favorite Artists Lisa?

Claude Monet an Eighteenth-century painter and the founder of impressionism and who is seen as a precursor to modernism. He painted what he seen with changing sea-sons. He has numerous paintings that show exquisite artistry. I thought he had that gift to capture the light and changing seasons.

He most certainly did and couldn't agree more.

Excuse me, let me take this call. Hello. Hollywood, I am downtown I'll see you tomorrow.

Don't worry about it.

She was inspirational to be around and her enthusiasm was catching even a fondness. When he laid eyes on her he felt an alluring force with charm. One of her qualities about her is she is recklessly bold. My mind was fixed on a friendship for now.

Blake, would you mind taking me home? Certainly, waiter check, please, Yes, Sir. They got up and left he opened the door for her.

It's a lovely night out, and the stars are bright, and the moon is right.

I had a wonderful time with you, Blake. Will you call me tomorrow? Absolutely. Blake headed home, sat down on the couch, and before he knew it, he awoke the next day.

He decided to give her a call the next day and ask her if she wanted to go to Mistral, a French Restaurant in New Jersey, so he did. Sure I will go. I'll make reservations for six thirty is that OK? Sure Lisa and I'll be over your house at five O'clock. I'll see you then, she said. He called and made the reservation. Sat down and watched a few Documentaries?

Claude Monet an Eighteenth-century painter and the founder of impressionist and who is seen as a precursor to modernism. He painted what he seen with changing seasons. He has numerous painting that are exquisite art, it wasn't long and then Hollywood called; perhaps I'll see him tomorrow he said. And then of all of a sudden there was a knock at the door from Amy.

Come in and make yourself at home. We will be leaving in a five minutes. Do you need anything? No I'm fine and looking forward to this drive in the country and talking with you.

Are you ready, perhaps we could take my car?

So we walked out, and he opened the door for here. He put some classical music on. So tell me, what have you been doing with yourself?

I'm finishing up my last year of Nursing College. Good for you an R.N. What a brilliant field that you major in. You certainly have a kind and caring personality in you.

I don't have a fear of it, but one thing is for sure it's real working among sick people. I worked for four years and waited to go to College with some money saved.

After that, I got a good job working part-time and making good money. I have knowledge of student loans and the interest that's outrageous. I agree, and right now, we are in an era of economic development and opportunities. Logistics and or commodities and fuel are all reasonable including housing. The scenery is beautiful and I never been to Princeton NJ. It's a fine restaurant. Do you like fish Amy? Yes, absolutely will you order for us. Sure sweetheart. What type of work do you do? I'm thinking about hauling stone out of a quarry, your home every day the pay is Ok. Right now I am running small commodities from North Philadelphia to Hollywood pa. Lisa we are here.

Tell me some more about that book at the dinner, table you were reading? it looks interesting. Let me open the door for you and welcome to Mistral. Thank you I have a reservation for two, your name Blake. Right this way sir. Thank You.

We'll have two French Martinis and for starters, shrimp, carrots and celery sauce dip-ping.

Sir, we also have the Duck leg non fit with a red wine reduction. I thought we could split it. Believe me you will be full. Tell me more about the book you were reading the other day?

Your Martinis sir, Thank you. What is going to be said, Amy concerns the natural evil and will apply to variations. Is it limited to ask and about? In every aspect it's reasonable, that makes a slight examination into the natural powers of the mind and to compare things in order to be recommended to us.

There is knowledge that reaches are negations, and, affirmations concerning ideas and issues have perhaps relation, coexistence, and real existence, and identity.

Your starter, Ladies and Gentleman, the food is good, and I want to thank you again; you were saying Blake?

The book gives a person a wider perspective of what is happening in the World and America, giving an understanding that can give a person to excel, achieve knowledge and a knowing. Seeing history repeating itself. Einstein: If you keep doing the same thing over and over again with the same results is insanity, furthermore, for your Constitution Rights.

Our Constitution is simple and practical and meets extraordinary needs, which is why our constitutional system must be an enduring political mechanism America has produced. It has met every vast expansion of territory of foreign wars and bitter inter-national rights and strife.

How is your meal? Good Thank You. It looks like our duck is coming out and they do a good job of cutting it up. Help yourself to some Duck, would you like me to order a bottle of wine? Please do.

Waiter, can I have a bottle of white Bordeaux, Perhaps the Chateau Huat Brion Blanc? Right away sir. That was fast he poured both of them a glass of wine.

So any way what were you saying and or knowledge or understanding? Yes, dear, it could be pertaining to the understanding or perception? There's intelligence in the quality of knowing of, understanding, knowledge, and wisdom. One of the qualities I like about you, Blake, is your intellectualism in Philosophy the Doctrine that all knowledge from the intellect. Thanks for sharing that sweetheart.

But anyway Amy what I'm also saying is hope that the normal balance of executive and legislative may be wholly adequate to meet the unprecedented task before us. But it is also said an unprecedented demand and action that is departing from the normal balance of procedure.

We face the arduous days that lie before us in national unity with the clear conscious of old and young moral values, which comes a clean and unclean satisfaction from others.

Blake was prepared under his Constitutional duty to recommend the measures of the Constitution to a stricken nation in the midst of stricken chaos. Those who cherish their freedom and recognize and respect the right s of their neighbors must work together to triumph of moral laws and principles in order for peace and justice must prevail.

But Corruption is a solidarity, an independence about America and the modern world both technically and morality, which makes it impossible for any nation to isolate itself from economic and political upheavals in the presence in the world, especially when the upheavals are spreading and not declining. The Five Faces of Corruption goes back thousands of years perhaps to Roman times. The faces are a face and not a face.

Even in China in the Ming Dynasty, they took away the Mandate of Heaven: The Mandate of Heaven was a religious belief among a lot of Chinese. Based on The stars, universe, karma, bees, trees, and streams all living aspects that God has given us.

Princess Dowager poisoned her nephew for Control. There were War Lords raiding, villages raping, robbing taking territory. Man has been fighting over territory since the ice age.

"Corruption by Old Age"

"Corruption by Clash of Cultures"

"Corruption by Tyranny"

"Corruption by Treachery"

"Corruption by Conquest"

Another example would be, in the Seventeenth Century, toward the evening, an Emperor died in a small town. He ruled a small country for fifty years. He was a bigoted and stern man, bent on to impose the Muslim Religion.

He wanted to make the lives of others who were not Muslims intolerable, so he spent the greater of his reign making war. He put his father in prison, and he also killed his older brother and anyone who felt threatened by his authority. His crimes were so numerous that while he was on his deathbed, he was forced by his conscious to comfort them. "I am so evil," he said. "I fear God will have no place for me. For that reason, bury me Beheaded, for they say for all those come bareheaded into God's presence will receive his mercy. But I do not believe he will look at me. His crimes came from his calculating spirit and his temperament which lead him to profit from himself. In fact, he was living in the most luxurious court upon his time. He had no feeling for people or understanding of popular movements. He allowed his Mughal courtiers a license: they practiced all kinds of sexual acts, took drugs and drank heavily, and they also bribed their way to office. Furthermore, they stole unashamedly from the Hindus. Whenever it pleased them, it took the woman and their possessions. One day he turned to one of his advisors and asked him, why are the Mahratta's rising up against us? He forgot that he was killing them for over a half-century because of his intense bigotry and his intolerance. On his deathbed, he told them to behead him so God would take him.

One of his greatest crimes was participating in similar circumstances around the World, and left his country weak and divided. And his Grandfather was not in the least concerned to find a common ground.

He would invite new punishments for the Hindus, and he told them to regard them as common slaves. Eventually, the British

Government stepped in.

They didn't do any better in Governing the State. They started to rob and take. But it wouldn't be long before they became their own country.

Blake's way of diversity and identity, as far as diversity, and identity, are existence of ideas or issues and are of agreement and disagreement. There may be an attempt of the skeptics to destroy reason and argument or is the scope of their disputes or inquiries. They journey to find objections both to reasoning and to abstract reasoning and to those who regard existence and matters of facts.

The main objective against all abstract reasoning comes from the idea of times. Ideas in the common life are very clear and intelligible. There could be a purpose to tame mankind over to shock common sense, or there is interference or a certain instant in our nature which is deceitful that circumstances, that may have been overlooked.

He will allow your premises, but he will deny your conclusion only because you might conclude reasoning has no influence in your life or because it shouldn't have any influence, or it may have no influence with knowledge.

They enter in an area with more dangers and in an area of confusion and is sometimes by passed about men who slip into mysterious regions with thought and design. They are trafficking with Death. His morality doesn't restrain him, so he moves at his own pace. All his moral issues have been resolved by the process of annihilating them. He is dedicated to corruption on a scale that is full. He is not content with small pickings and of an honest living.

He wants the whole population at his mercy and also wants at any price is power and wealth to defend against all comers.

Of course he knows he is danger, but danger arouses him to greater feats. He has passed the stage where he can measure danger and also takes the right precautions. It's a Ghost he can brush away with his hands. But a kind of prolonged stupefaction sets in. Therefore, some of the ordinary familiar things of daily life become unreal to him. For him it's nothing to give orders to kill people. There are points of catastrophe, of course surprises happen.

The corrupt man protests his innocence so he says he has done everything for his cause and or for his people. He tells the public his arrest will be in history. He may say at the very worst, I have been to trustful of my subordinates. Sometimes guilt and punishment set in. In some cases, he's defenseless he summons his morality to his side.

Adolf Hitler was a prejudiced man of all types of women, men and children. But he proclaimed he had to fight the greatest War in history because it was forced on him. Some catastrophes have an effect that changes their character. There is a return to moral principles, an effort to employ morality against their accusers and this is done almost mindlessly.

For some, they search for their extremity for a point of strength. And they look in the Bible, which they have disobeyed.

The murders that he committed by his Army and the circumstances are not difficult to assess. So memoirs are written in some cases to prove he has done nothing wrong. This is all unavailing. For thousands of years, the Church has recognized that penitence alone absolves the criminal? He must Plea for forgiveness from God. This rarely happens, so he is more likely to do Jail time, or hang himself and, or put a bullet in his head. In this case, he poisons himself because they are going to kill him.

The integrity of the Moral code to some is Dignity, Constitution, and the utility of History. If were to lower or depreciate currency for the sake of success, rank, or reputation we may debase for the sake of man's influence or of his party, Religion, and of his good cause, which prospers by his credit and which suffers by his disgrace.

Awaken by the dangers which menace our freedom and prosperity we still retain the right and courage to exercise our Constitutional Rights and sovereign control over the Government. In order to destroy the economic and political power of Inflation, Stagflation and political power over Government regulations, which has come between us?

A nation that forgets its past has no future. The Understanding of learning about your history is not about making any one person or people of a group feel guilty. You cannot be guilty of actions that took place before you were born.

It was Blake's, purpose that the process of peace, if they begin, shall be open, and that shall involve and permit henceforth no secret understandings of any kind. The day of conquest is upon us, so is also the day of secret covenants that have entered into the interest of Government and likely some unlooked moment to upset our peace with Subversion tactics: The act of subverting the state of being subverted, especially a systematic attempt to overthrow or undermine the Constitution and or our Government or political system by persons working from within. There will be no peace.

What should be pledged to a complete house cleaning or an investigation in the Department of Justice and Congress and the Department of executive departments.

We demand the power of the Federal Government is to be crushed of its faults and restrictions.

We should be pledged to Self-sufficient and recover Coal, Oil reserves and Pipelines, which is being fraudulently intervened. That is being wrongfully transferred to the Government's private interests. And the complete revision of the water-power Act. We favor public ownership or the nations power and creator and development of a national superpower system to supply at a cost light and to supply the farmers and control of all are natural resources, including coal and other iron and ores, oils, and timbers.

We declare a favorable railroad law and the fixing of railroad rates upon the basis of actual, prudent investments and cost of service and against bureaucratic control as one way of solution and favor reduction of Federal Taxes upon individual incomes and legitimate businesses, limiting tax extractions to the requirements of the People, submitting to the people, for your judgment, a constitutional amendment providing Congress may be acting a statue and make it over a judicial veto.

We favor drastic innovation on the duties of manufactures. The reconstruction of the Federal Reserve and Federal Loan systems, not illuminated by control like speculators and international finance, and to make the credit of the nation fair terms without dis-crimination to businesses, college tuition, Interest rates, and to White and Blue collar worker's healthcare workers or heroes. We demand that the Interstate Commerce commission to proceed forthwith by any approximation to pre-war levels as an increase, including all logistics. We favor Tax cuts with utilities, property State sales tax and food taxes. Furthermore, increases in Social security, Social Supplemental income, and Socials Disability.

We denounce the Socialism system of America and foreign policy under recent administrations in the interests of foreign policy and political gain by subversion tactics and by financial imperialists.

We do not favor foreign oil monopolists and international bankers and bakers, which at times it degrades our State Department from its high service, as a kind of intermediary as defenseless to the poor and middle class to a trading outpost for those interests and seekers engaged in the exploitation of weaker driven into poorness as the contrary to the will of the Government, destructive of domestic development and provocative of war. The process of degeneration and decay in Government is always terrible, and the decay of a nation is more terrible than the corruption of the physical body.

What things are worse is the harm that is being done to the people. They didn't ask that their society is dying or should be reduced to a kind of ignominious death-in-life. Corruption has worked on the Historical forces over which they have control, that has seeped down through the government or it has brought about subversion from within. That arises from the unattainable cultural elements in society. Tyranny, Treachery, Conquest, Clash of Cultures, and the Old Age that bring about corrupt societies that exist. Ask what your country is doing for you, and then ask yourself what you are doing for your country?

For some, their eyes are closed to the fact there is something more than a mere form of government by which we are restrained from freedom and orderly life—our Constitution, which really rests on the faith of ballot boxes.

Any nation that refuses their right to exercise forbearance and respect their freedom can no longer remain strong and retain the confidence and respect of others.

My knowledge in diversity, knowledge and history as far as some ideas could be in the way of agreement and disagreement of ideas or truth. There may be an attempt to the skeptics by argument, or is the scope of their disputes and inquiries. I will allow your premises but deny your conclusion.

Perhaps it has to be done in a process with constructing of placing together a view or in juxtaposition of things in the same category or class that which is widely differing from each other in order to render the more widely marked.

Thank you, are you ready, sweetheart? Yes Blake, I would like to say the dinner and listening to you were a fascinating. I never knew you were well-versed in worldly issues at the present time.

Thank you, I am glad you enjoyed the restaurant. It is somewhat of a picturesque place, but even in picturesque places, the soil has been corrupted with problems and crime. Are you ready for a nice drive home? Of course, thank you.

Waiter, check, please. Yes, sir.

Dear.

Thank you for opening the door for me. You are welcome, and it's a nice day out.

The food was delicious. Yes, it was. Do you have a preference of music? Is anything good? It's a wonderful thing the trees and breeze and all other things to see. Amy, will you be graduating from College? Shortly do you have any plans of staying in Philadelphia? I am not sure there is an opportunity in my field. The good news the debt is little. I'm thinking about moving up to the Northeast. The city is getting worse. That's the truth; in fact, a lot of millennials are moving out because of crime.

It's ironic you asked me that question. What is becoming of us, Blake? I am unsure. I haven't thought about it yet. I'm trying to think. Would you tell me the truth? Of course.

Are you seeing another woman? Absolutely not, my dear. I believe you. There have been some tragedies in my life at an early age. Friendship is a nice way to start out with excitement and mystery.

He thought about her for a few minutes and still didn't know. She's a mystery and willingness. It seems to me that she is not like other people. There are many things she has and one is kindness, with conscious with other qualities. You can only understand people if you can feel them. I also felt that connection. The moment He thought about her his feelings go into brightness. He suspected what she wanted and wasn't after anything. And she was healthy and exciting to talk to.

The ride is lovely out today, Blake. I have been meaning to ask you. The Claude Monet exhibition is coming to The Art Museum, would you like to go shortly? Of course, he is one of my favorite painters from the Eighteenth century the founder of impressionists. It sounds like a plan; I'll make the arrangements.

Melisa, have you ever been to New Hope? No, I can't say I have. It has an interesting History; It's located for a rest stop between Philadelphia and New York. Upper bucks County. It's a small town with an area of 1.42 square miles. It sits on the other side from New Jersey and there's a steel bridge where you can walk over. It's more of a tourist town you have to park your car and walk through. There's a Theater, fine dining, sweet shops, Antique places and or all types of Artistic places. you would like it.

It sounds just fantastic Blake. We are almost at your place. Let me pull up to park. I had a good time and I hope I will see you again, Blake. Let me open your door for you. She grabbed me and kissed me on the cheek and said thank you. But she said don't go dear and don't go know my love, I can teach you, I will teach you. I know your sheets are silk. I want you to feel togetherness. I grabbed her hand and kissed the back of it, and said I have to take care of some things. Her faced seemed fresh and bright when he told her he would call her later.

Blake was tired and decided to just take it easy, and just about when he was going to sit down on his chair. He got a phone call that someone in the neighborhood was get-ting a small shipment of marijuana in. He couldn't tell you what happened only there were rumors that the guy climbed up the back of the house like some cat and it disappeared. At this point The money was running low and eventually Hollywood's money isn't go to last forever either. What Blake was foreseeing this is not a life.

He sat down and was running ideas through his head about going back to work or driving trucks. He had class A with experienced in more than one kind. There were openings all over. There was an opening up at a trucking company hauling stone out of quarry.

Hello, what's up Hollywood? No he said Blake can't go down this time of night. He be over first thing in the morning say around 10 O'clock. See you tomorrow. He called it an early night and went to bed.

When Blake awoke he jumped in the shower and shaved. Decide to make home fries, two eggs over and boiled pieces of asparagus in water with orange juice, milk, and toast. Peeled the potatoes and sliced them and put them in a pan with a little oil. Took out another pan filled it halfway with wither and added the asparagus.

He sat down and had a nice breakfast. Went and read some of the newspaper, nothing more dramatic other than the T.V.

Blake gave Hollywood a call and told him he was on his way. Drove up and he gave the money to him.

Blake went down and got the usual amount of Cocaine for 300.00 dollars and went back and delivered it. The Kensington Strangler was all over the media.

Blake decided to go over the Flea's and shoot some pool, ping pong, and darts and listen to some music. Go down the dungeon. Got a few beers starting playing darts, switched occasional to ping pong,

I miss playing as often as I use to with a worthy opponent.

The '80s. was also a vision of floating disco balls, neon lights, and small glass mirrors covered in the finest Colombian flake. You hear the slamming of bathroom stalls, snorting, sniffling, and the slapping bass of funk. You think of the heads of the major cocaine cartels. But few think of the "Yuppie Conspiracy," the only cocaine enterprise brought down by one funk song.

Blake decided to give Melissa a call to see if she wanted to go out to Dinner. Hey Sweetheart would you be interested in going to a fine German Restaurant? The Austria Village in Rockledge. Absolutely I'll be up at 7 O'clock. They have a nice family, friend-ly small restaurant. I'll see you at my place. He stayed over The Wolf-man's house for a little longer had a few more beers. They were good hobbies to pick up at an early age. I left some hours later to get ready to meet Melissa.

Drove home cleaned up a little and took a shower and got dressed for dinner. It was more than a minute or two before I heard a knock at the door. How are you? Come on in. How is school going? Fine it won't be long before I am on my way to a secure future. Its right up the road The A.V. we'll be there in 5 minutes.

What do you recommend? The Veal with mashed potatoes and corn. Would you like a salad? No, Thank you.

Time really goes by let me park. They entered and sat down and ordered. Blake it seems like uncertainty in America at times. There are a lot of variables: loans, interest rates, car financing and gas prices, and a mortgage.

How was dinner? Very good would like to walk over to the bar and have some drinks and talk? Sure why not?

Yes, things are difficult with America's issues. People were in a frantic with the Bombings. He got caught and, most likely by opening up his mouth. You cannot let things stop you.

The so-called Unabomber who attacked academics, businessmen and random civilians with homemade bombs from 1978 killing three people and injuring 23 with the stated goal of fomenting the collapse of the modern social order — a violent spree that ended.

Alone in a shack in the Montana wilderness, he fashioned homemade bombs and launched a violent one-man campaign to destroy industrial society. The Unabomber was flanked by federal agents as he was led from the federal courthouse in Helena, Mont.

In the public eye, he fused two styles of violence: the periodic targeting of the demented serial killer, and the ideological fanaticism of the terrorist.

Victims railed against commentators who took seriously a 35,000-word manifesto that he had written to justify his actions and evangelize the ideas that he claimed inspired them. Psychologists involved in the trial saw his writing as evidence of schizophrenia. His lawyers tried to mount an insanity defense and sought to represent himself in court, risking execution to do so; his lawyers said that that was yet further evidence of insanity.

Years before the manifesto was published, he had no reputation beyond that of a twisted reveler in violence, picking victims seemingly at random, known only by a mysterious-sounding nickname with roots in the F.B.I.'s investigation into him: "the Unabomber." It became widely publicized that some of his victims lost their fingers while opening a package bomb. Simply going through the mail prompted flickers of nervousness in many Americans.

After his arrest, his biography emerged. He had scored 167 on an I.Q. test as a boy and entered Harvard at 16. In graduate school at the University of Michigan, he worked in a field of mathematics so esoteric that a member of his dissertation committee estimated that only 10 or 12 people in the country understood it. By 25, he was an assistant professor at the University of California, Berkeley.

Then he dropped out — not just from Berkeley, but from civilization. Starting in 1971 and continuing until his arrest, he lived in a shack he built himself in rural Montana. He forsook running water, read by the light of homemade candles, stopped filing federal tax returns and subsisted on rabbits. A ramshackle, nondescript cabin in the middle of a woods.

He argued that damage to the environment and the alienating effects of foreign technology were so heinous that the social and industrial underpinnings of modern life should be destroyed.

A vast majority of Americans determined that the Unabomber must be a psychopath the moment they heard of him, and while he was front-page news, his text did not generally find receptive readers outside a tiny fringe of the environmental movement. The term "Unabomber" entered popular discourse as shorthand for the type of brainy misfit who might harbor terrifying impulses.

His manifesto accorded centrality to a healthy environment without mentioning global warming; it warned about the dangers of people becoming "dependent" on technology while making scant reference to the internet. To young people afflicted by social media anomie and fearful of climate doom.

His infamous label came from "UNABOM," the F.B.I.'s code for university and airline bombing. That designation was inspired by his first targets, from 1978 to 1980: academics at Northwestern University, the president of United Airlines and the passengers of a flight from Chicago to Washington. The victims suffered cuts, burns and smoke inhalation. The authorities were aided in connecting several early attacks by the fact that the mysterious initials "FC" had been engraved on the bombs or spray-painted near the explosions.

The Unabomber struck one to four times a year for most years until 1987, when he left a bomb at a computer store in Salt Lake City. A woman remembered making eye con-tact with the man who had dropped off the package that later exploded, and soon a sketch was publicized of a mustachioed suspect wearing sunglasses and a hoodie.

Some years passed without an attack. Then, the Unabomber struck twice in the same week.

Packages containing bombs arrived at the home of a geneticist at the University of California San Francisco and at the office of David Gelernter, a computer scientist at Yale University. Each man lost multiple fingers.

He sustained permanent hearing loss, whose office burst into flames, bled nearly to the point of death, and lost much of the vision in his right eye.

Lisa, are you in the mood for some custard? Yes, please. I know a good spot up the street; the place is called the custard stand. Do you like colored or like the rainbow sprinkles. Blake I am glad I can talk to you about anything. Let's park and go inside and have a treat. We walked in and sat down.

Blake, I was just curious about your opinion on Global Warming or Climate change?

There is a reason why it remains unquiet and restless even if there is regard to skepticism because it is driven by contradictions. It is clear, that a distinct idea can contain circumstances contradictory to itself or to another distinct idea? Is it comprehensible and absurd as any proposition, which can be formed? There is skepticism that arises from some of this paradoxical.

Is it limited to ask or about? In every respect, it's reasonable that suffices to make an examination into the natural powers of the mind and to compare things in order to be recommended to us. There are subjects of Science, History, innovation, and Moral conduct.

Despite the scientific census on Climate change, proof has been shown that scientists and intuitions that were involved were in a global conspiracy or engaged in a manipulative hoax. More allegations surfaced of mal practice most notably in (The Climate research unit with Email Controversy) (Climate Gate)

The Climate Gate also claims that researchers faked research to their publication to suppress their critics.

The bottom line is pollution Carbon Dioxide, food, Non-ferries and Ferries metals, plastics, fertilizers, mercury, Propane, Fluorine, methane, chlorines, HFC, HCFC, CFC,11,12, and 13 and residual wastes, even cow farts and humans. Climate change is a conflict-ual having underground sea thermal activities.

And it goes beyond to automobiles and airplanes. Aviation fuels are petroleum-based fuels, or petroleum and synthetic fuel blends, used to power aircraft. They have more stringent requirements than fuels used for ground use, such as heating and road transport, and contain additives to enhance or maintain properties important to fuel performance or handling. They are kerosene-based (JP-8 and Jet A-1) for gas turbine-powered aircraft. Piston-engine aircraft use leaded gasoline and those with diesel engines may use jet fuel (kerosene). The U.S. Air Force had been certified to use a 50-50 blend of kerosene and synthetic fuel derived from coal or natural gas as a way of stabilizing the cost of fuel.

Specific energy (energy per unit mass) is an important criterion in selecting fuel for an aircraft.

Hydrocarbon fuels' much higher energy storage capability than batteries has so far prevented electric aircraft from using electric batteries as the main propulsion energy store, becoming viable for smallest personal aircrafts.

No one talks about Trash to Steam. Do you think it's Global warming and or Climate change? Or Pollution in the Troposphere? The Troposphere starts from the ground up and goes seven miles up.

Global Warming or the greenhouse effect is supposedly not a

different concept that leads to heating the earth that's supposedly melting the Ice-burgs. However, Global Warming is being going on for thousands of ages and so have the Icebergs.

There is also Theory the earths moved off its axis 3 degrees, what say you? Hurricanes and storms have been going on for thousands of years. Don't misunderstand me there is no doubt that the sun rays are interfering in the Troposphere and or what's more furthermore pollution.

Glacial stages in North America and or the Last Glacial Period in the semiarid Andes around Aconcagua and Tupungato

This article is about glacial periods in general. For specific recent glacial periods often referred to as the "Ice Age", see Last Glacial Period, Pleistocene, and Quaternary glaciation. For other uses, see Ice age (disambiguation).

An ice age is a long period of reduction in the temperature of Earth's surface and atmosphere, resulting in the presence or expansion of continental and polar ice sheets and alpine glaciers. Earth's climate alternates between ice ages and greenhouse periods, during which there are no glaciers on the planet. Earth is currently in the ice age called Quaternary glaciation. Individual pulses of cold climate within an ice age are termed glacial periods (or, alternatively, glacial, glaciations, glacial stages, stadia's, stades, or colloquially, ice ages), and intermittent warm periods within an ice age are called interglacial or interstadials.

In glaciology, ice age implies the presence of extensive ice sheets in the northern and southern hemispheres. By this definition, Earth is in an interglacial period—the Holocene. The amount of anthropogenic greenhouse gases emitted into Earth's oceans and atmosphere is projected to delay the next glacial period, which otherwise would begin in around 50,000 years, by between 100,000 and 500,000 years.

In 1742 (1706–1767), an engineer and geographer living in Geneva visited the valley of Chamonix in the Alps of Savoy. Two years later, he published an account of his journey. He reported that the inhabitants of that valley attributed the dispersal of erratic boulders to the glaciers, saying that they had once extended much farther. Later, similar explanations were reported from other regions of the Alps. In 1815 the carpenter and chamois hunter (1767–1858) explained erratic boulders in the Val de Bagnes in the Swiss canton of Valais as being due to glaciers previously extending further. An unknown woodcutter from Meringa in the Bernese advocated a similar idea in a discussion with the Swiss-German geologist between (1786–1855) made comparable explanations are also known from the Val de Ferret in the Valais and the Sea land in western Switzerland and in Goethe's scientific work. Such explanations could also be found in other parts of the world. When the Bavarian naturalist between (1806 and 1878) visited the Chilean Andes in 1849–1850, the natives attributed fossil moraines to the former action of glaciers.

Meanwhile, European scholars had begun to wonder what had caused the dispersal of erratic material. From the middle of the 18th century, some discussed ice as a means of transport. The Swedish mining expert in (1712–1772) was, in 1742, the first person to suggest drifting sea ice was a cause of the presence of erratic boulders in the

Scandinavian and Baltic regions. [ In 1795, the Scottish philosopher and gentleman naturalist James Hutton (1726–1797) explained erratic boulders in the Alps by the action of glaciers. Two decades later, in 1818, the Swedish botanist in (1780–1851) published his theory of a glaciation of the Scandinavian peninsula. He regarded glaciation as a regional phenomenon.

Only a few years later, the Danish-Norwegian geologist Jens Esmark argued for a sequence of worldwide ice ages. In a paper published in 1824, Esmark proposed changes in climate as the cause of those glaciations. He attempted to show that they originated from changes in Earth's orbit. Esmark discovered the similarity between moraines near Haukalivatnet Lake near sea level in Rogaland and moraines at branches of Jostedalsbreen. Esmark's discoveries were later attributed to or appropriated by The-odor Kjerulf and Louis Agassiz.

During the following years, Esmark's ideas were discussed and taken over in parts by Swedish, Scottish, and German scientists.

At the University of Edinburgh, Robert Jameson (1774–1854) seemed to be relatively open to Esmark's ideas, as reviewed by a Norwegian professor of glaciology remarked that ancient glaciers in Scotland were most probably prompted by Esmark. In Germany, a geologist and professor of forestry at an academy in Dreissigacker (since incorporated in the southern Thuringian city of Meiningen), adopted.

Esmark's theory. In a paper published in 1832, Bernhardi speculated about the polar ice caps, once reaching as far as the temperate zones of the globe.

Agassiz appears to have been already familiar with Bernhardi's paper at that time. At the beginning of 1837, Schimper coined the term "ice age" ("Eiszeit") for the period of the glaciers. In July 1837 Agassiz presented their synthesis before the annual meeting of the Swiss Society for Natural Research at Neuchâtel. The audience was very critical, and some were opposed to the new theory because it contradicted the established opinions on climatic history. Most contemporary scientists thought that Earth had been gradually cooling down since its birth as a molten globe.

In order to persuade the skeptics, Agassiz embarked on geological fieldwork. He published his book Study on Glaciers ("Études sur les glaciers") in 1840. Charpentier was put out by this, as he had also been preparing a book about the glaciation of the Alps. Charpentier felt that Agassiz should have given him precedence as it was he who had introduced Agassiz to in-depth glacial research. As a result of personal quarrels, Agassiz had also omitted any mention of Schimper in his book.

It took several decades before the Ice Age theory was fully accepted by scientists. This happened on an international scale in the second half of the 1870s, following the work of James Croll, including the publication of Climate and Time in Their Geological Relations in 1875, which provided a credible explanation for the causes of ice ages.

There is evidence and there are three main types of evidence for ice ages: geological, chemical, and paleontological and the.

Geological evidence for ice ages comes in various forms, including rock scouring and scratching, glacial moraines, drumlins, valley cutting, and the deposition of till or tillites and glacial erratic. Successive glaciations tend to distort and erase the geological evidence for earlier glaciations, making it difficult to interpret. Furthermore, this evidence was difficult to date exactly; early theories assumed that the glaciers were short compared to the long inter-glacial. The advent of sediment and ice cores revealed the true situation: glacials are long, inter-glacials. It took some time for the current theory to be worked out.

The chemical evidence mainly consists of variations in the ratios of isotopes in fossils present in sediments and sedimentary rocks and ocean sediment cores. For the most recent glacial periods, ice cores provide climate proxies, both from the ice itself and from atmospheric samples provided by included bubbles of air. Because water containing lighter isotopes has a lower heat of evaporation, its proportion decreases with warmer conditions. This allows a temperature record to be constructed. This evidence can be confounded, however, by other factors recorded by isotope ratios.

The paleontological evidence consists of changes in the geographical distribution of fossils. During a glacial period, cold-adapted organisms spread into lower latitudes, and organisms that prefer warmer conditions become extinct or retreat into lower latitudes. This evidence is also difficult to interpret because it requires sequences of sediments covering a long period of time, over a wide range of latitudes and which are easily correlated; ancient organisms that survive for several million years without change and whose temperature preferences are easily diagnosed; and

The was finding of the relevant fossils. Despite the difficulties, analysis of ice core and ocean sediment cores has provided a credible record of glacials and inter-glacials over the past few million years. These also confirm the linkage between ice ages and continental crust phenomena such as glacial moraines, drumlins, and glacial erratic. Hence, the continental crust phenomena are accepted as good evidence of earlier ice ages when they are found in layers created much earlier than the time range for which ice cores and ocean sediment cores are available.

Major ice ages. There have been at least five major ice ages in Earth's history (the An-dean-Saharan, late Paleozoic, and the latest Quaternary Ice Age). Outside these ages, Earth was previously thought to have been ice-free even in high latitudes; such periods are known as greenhouse periods. However, other studies dispute this, finding evidence of occasional glaciations at high latitudes even during apparent greenhouse periods.

Rocks from the earliest well-established ice age called the Herodian, that's been dated around 2.4 to 2.1 billion years ago during the early Proterozoic Eon. Several hundreds of kilometers of the Herodian Super group are exposed 10 to 100 kilometers (6 to 62 mi) north of the north shore of Lake Huron, extending from near Sault Ste. Marie to Sudbury, northeast of Lake Huron, with giant layers of now-lithified till beds, drop stones, outwash, and scoured basement rocks. Correlative Herodian deposits have been found near Marquette, Michigan, and a correlation has been made with Paleoproterozoic glacial deposits from Western Australia. The

Herodian ice age was caused by atmospheric methane, a greenhouse gas, during the Great Oxygenation Event.

The next well-documented ice age, and probably the most severe of the last billion years, occurred from 720 to 630 million years ago (the Cryogen Ian period) and may have produced a Snowball Earth in which glacial ice sheets reached the equator, possibly being ended by the accumulation of greenhouse gases such as CO2 produced by volcanoes. "The presence of ice on the continents and pack ice on the oceans would inhibit both silicate weathering and photosynthesis, which are the two major sinks for CO2 at present." It has been suggested that the end of this ice age was responsible for the subsequent Ediacaran and Cambrian explosions, though this model is recent and controversial.

The Andean-Saharan occurred from 460 to 420 million years ago, during the Late Ordovician and the Silurian period. Sediment records show the fluctuating sequences of glacials and inter-glacials during the last several million years.

The evolution of land plants at the onset of the Devonian period caused a long-term increase in planetary oxygen levels and a reduction of CO2 levels, which resulted in the late Paleozoic icehouse. Its former name, the Karoo glaciation, was named after the glacial tills found in the Karoo region of South Africa. There were extensive polar ice caps at intervals from 360 to 260 million years ago in South Africa during the Carboniferous and early Permian periods. Correlatives are known from Argentina, also in the center of the ancient supercontinent Gondwanaland.

Although the Mesozoic Era retained a greenhouse climate over its timespan and was previously assumed to have been entirely glaciation-free, more recent studies suggest that brief periods of glaciation occurred in both hemispheres during the Early Cretaceous. Geologic and palaeoclimatological records suggest the existence of glacial periods during the Valanginian, Hauterivian, and Aptian stages of the Early Cretaceous. Ice-rafted glacial drop stones indicate that in the Northern Hemisphere, ice sheets may have extended as far south as the Iberian Peninsula during the Hauterivian and Aptian. Although ice sheets largely disappeared from Earth for the rest of the period (potential reports from the Turonian, otherwise the warmest period of the Phanerozoic, are disputed), ice sheets and associated sea ice appear to have briefly returned to Antarctica near the very end of the Maastrichtian just prior to the Cretaceous-Paleogene extinction event.

The definition of the Quaternary as beginning 2.58 Ma is based on the formation of the Arctic ice cap. The Antarctic ice sheet began to form earlier, at about 34 Ma, in the mid-Cenozoic (Eocene-Oligocene Boundary). The term Late Cenozoic Ice Age is used to include this early phase.

Ice ages can be further divided by location and time; for example, in (180,000–130,000 years) and Würm (70,000–10,000 years) refer specifically to glaciation in the Alpine region. The maximum extent of the ice is not maintained for the full interval. The scouring action of each glaciation tends to remove most of the evidence of prior ice sheets almost completely, except in regions where the later sheet does not achieve full coverage. Glacials and inter-glacials and the Glacial period and Interglacial perhaps show the pattern of temperature and ice volume changes associated with recent glacials and inter-glacials with minimum and maximum glaciation.

Glacial is characterized by cooler and drier climates over most of Earth and large land and sea ice masses extending outward from the poles. Mountain glaciers in otherwise unglaciated areas extend to lower elevations due to a lower snow line. Sea levels drop due to the removal of large volumes of water above sea level in the icecaps. There is evidence that ocean circulation patterns are disrupted by glaciations. The glacials and inter-glacials coincide with changes in orbital forcing of climate due to Milankovitch cycles, which are periodic changes in Earth's orbit and the tilt of Earth's rotational axis.

Earth has been in an interglacial period known as the Holocene for around 11,700 years, and an article in Nature argues that it might be most analogous to a previous interglacial that lasted 28,000 years. Predicted changes in orbital forcing suggest that the next glacial period would begin at least 50,000 years from now. Moreover, anthropogenic forcing from increased greenhouse gases is estimated to potentially outweigh the orbital forcing of the Milankovitch cycles for hundreds of thousands of years.

Some Feedback processes each glacial period is subject to positive feedback, which makes it more severe, and negative feedback, which mitigates. The Positive is an important form of feedback is provided by Earth's albedo, which is how much of the sun's energy is reflected rather than absorbed by Earth. Ice and snow increase Earth's albedo, while forests reduce its albedo. When the air temperature decreases, ice and snow fields grow, and they reduce forest cover. This continues until competition with a negative feedback mechanism forces the system to an equilibrium.

One theory is that when glaciers form, two things happen: the ice grinds rocks into dust, and the land becomes dry and arid. This allows winds to transport iron rich dust into the open ocean, where it acts as a fertilizer that causes massive algal blooms that pull large amounts of CO2 out of the atmosphere. This in turn, makes it even colder and causes the glaciers to grow more.

In 1956, Professors hypothesized that an ice-free Arctic Ocean leads to increased snowfall at high latitudes. When low-temperature ice covers the Arctic Ocean, there is little evaporation or sublimation, and the polar regions are quite dry in terms of precipitation, comparable to the amount found in mid-latitude deserts. This low precipitation allows high-latitude snowfalls to melt during the summer. The ice-free Arctic Ocean absorbs solar radiation during the long summer days and evaporates more water into the Arctic atmosphere. With higher precipitation, portions of this snow may not melt during the summer and so glacial ice can form at lower altitudes and more southerly latitudes, reducing the temperatures over land by increased albedo as noted above. Furthermore, under this hypothesis, the lack of oceanic pack ice allows the increased exchange of waters between the Arctic and the North Atlantic Oceans, warming the Arctic and cooling the North Atlantic. Additional fresh water flowing into the North Atlantic during a warming cycle may also reduce the global ocean water circulation. Such a reduction (by reducing the effects of the Gulf Stream) would have a cooling effect on northern Europe, which in turn would lead to increased low-latitude snow retention during the summer. It has also been suggested by whom?] that during an extensive glacial, glaciers may move through the Gulf of Saint Lawrence, extending into the North Atlantic Ocean far enough to block the Gulf Stream.

There could be a negative: Ice sheets that form during glaciations erode the land beneath them. This can reduce the land area above sea level and thus diminish the amount of space on which ice sheets can form. This mitigates the albedo feedback, as does the rise in sea level that accompanies the reduced area of ice sheets, since the open ocean has a lower albedo than land.

Another negative feedback mechanism is the increased aridity occurring with glacial maxima, which reduces the precipitation available to maintain glaciation. The glacial retreat induced by this or any other process can be amplified by similar inverse positive feedbacks as for glacial advances.

According to research published in Nature Geoscience, human emissions of carbon dioxide (CO2) will defer the next glacial period. Researchers used data on Earth's orbit to find the historical warm interglacial period that looks most like the current one and from this, have predicted that the next glacial period would usually begin within 1,500 years. They go on to predict that emissions have been so high that it will not.

The causes of ice ages are not fully understood for either the large-scale ice age periods or the smaller ebb and flow of glacial-interglacial periods within an ice age. The consensus is that several factors are important: atmospheric composition, such as the concentrations of carbon dioxide and methane (the specific levels of the previously mentioned gases are now able to be seen with the new ice core samples from the European Project for Ice Coring in Antarctica (EPICA) Dome C in Antarctica over the past 800,000 years); changes in Earth's orbit around the Sun known as Milankovitch cycles; the motion of tectonic plates resulting in changes in the relative location and amount of continental and oceanic crust on Earth's surface, which affect wind and ocean cur-rents; variations in solar output; the orbital dynamics of the Earth–Moon system; the impact of relatively large meteorites and volcanism including eruptions of super volcanoes.

Some of these factors influence each other. For example, changes in Earth's atmospheric composition (especially the concentrations of greenhouse gases) may alter the climate, while climate change itself can change the atmospheric composition (for example, by changing the rate at which weathering removes CO2).

William and others propose that the Tibetan and Colorado Plateaus are immense CO2 "scrubbers" with a capacity to remove enough CO2 from the global atmosphere to be a significant causal factor of the 40 million-year Cenozoic Cooling trend. They further claim that approximately half of their uplift (and CO2 "scrubbing" capacity) occurred in the past 10 million years.

There are Changes in Earth's Troposphere and that's Pollution.

There is evidence that greenhouse gas levels fell at the start of ice ages and rose during the retreat of the ice sheets, but it is difficult to establish cause and effect. Greenhouse gas levels may also have been affected by other factors which have been proposed as causes of ice ages, such as the movement of continents and volcanism.

The Snowball Earth hypothesis maintains that the severe freezing in the late Proterozoic was ended by an increase in CO2 levels in the atmosphere, mainly from volcanoes, and some supporters of Snowball Earth argue that it was caused in the first place by a reduction in atmospheric CO2. The hypothesis also warns of future Snowball Earths.

Further evidence was provided that changes in solar insolation provide the initial trigger for Earth to warm after an Ice Age, with secondary factors like increases in greenhouse gases accounting for the magnitude of the change.

The position of the continents and the geological record appear to show that ice ages start when the continents are in positions that block or reduce the flow of warm water from the equator to the poles and thus allow ice sheets to form. The ice sheets increase Earth's reflectivity and thus reduce the absorption of solar radiation. With less radiation absorbed, the atmosphere cools; the cooling allows the ice sheets to grow, which further increases reflectivity in a positive feedback loop. The ice age continues until the reduction in weathering causes an increase in the greenhouse effect.

There are three main contributors to the layout of the continents that obstruct the movement of warm water to the poles.

A continent does sit on top of a pole, as Antarctica does today.

A polar sea is almost land-locked, as the Arctic Ocean is today.

A supercontinent covers most of the equator, as Rodinia did during the Cryogenian period.

Since today's Earth has a continent over the South Pole and an almost land-locked ocean over the North Pole, geologists believe that Earth will continue to experience glacial periods in the geologically near future.

Some scientists believe that the Himalayas are a major factor in the current ice age, because these mountains have increased Earth's total rainfall and therefore the rate at which carbon dioxide is washed out of the atmosphere, decreasing the greenhouse effect. The Himalayas' formation started about 70 million years ago when the Indo-Australian Plate collided with the Eurasian Plate, and the Himalayas are still rising by about 5 mm per year because the Indo-Australian plate is still moving at 67 mm/year. The history of the Himalayas broadly fits the long-term decrease in Earth's average temperature since the mid-Eocene, 40 million years ago.

Fluctuations in ocean currents could play an important contribution to ancient climate regimes is the variation of ocean currents, which are modified by continent position, sea levels and salinity, as well as other factors. They have the ability to cool (e.g. aid-ing the creation of Antarctic ice) and the ability to warm (e.g. giving the British Isles a temperate as opposed to a boreal climate). The closing of the Isthmus of Panama about 3 million years ago may have ushered in the present period of strong glaciation over North America by ending the exchange of water between the tropical Atlantic and Pacific Oceans.

The analyses suggest that ocean current fluctuations can adequately account for re-cent glacial oscillations. During the last glacial period the sea-level has fluctuated 20–30 m as water was sequestered, primarily in the Northern Hemisphere ice sheets. When ice collected and the sea level dropped sufficiently, flow through the Bering Strait (the narrow strait between Siberia and Alaska is about 50 m deep today) was reduced from erosion and resulting in increased flow from the North Atlantic. This realigned the thermohaline circulation in the Atlantic, increasing heat transport into the Arctic, which melted the polar ice accumulation and reduced other continental ice sheets. The release of water raised sea levels again, restoring the ingress of colder water from the Pacific with an accompanying shift to northern hemisphere ice accumulation.

According to a study published in all glacial periods of ice ages over the last 1.5 million years were associated with northward shifts of melting Antarctic icebergs which changed ocean circulation patterns, leading to more CO2 being pulled out of the atmosphere. The authors suggest that this process may be disrupted in the future as the Southern Ocean will become too warm for the icebergs to travel far enough to trigger these changes.

The Uplift of the Tibetan plateau and a geological theory of Ice Age development was suggested by the existence of an ice sheet covering the Tibetan Plateau during the Ice Ages (Last Glacial Maximum?). According to the plate-tectonic uplift of Tibet past the snow-line has led to a surface of c. 2,400,000 square kilometers (930,000 sq. mi) changing from bare land to ice with a 70% greater albedo. The reflection of energy into space resulted in a global cooling, triggering the Pleistocene Ice Age. Because this highland is at a subtropical latitude, with 4 to 5 times the insolation of high-latitude areas, what would be Earth's strongest heating surface has turned into a cooling sur-face.

As Scientists explains the interglacial periods by the 100,000-year cycle of radiation changes due to variations in Earth's orbit. This comparatively insignificant warming, when combined with the lowering of the Nordic inland ice areas and Tibet due to the weight of the superimposed ice-load, has led to the repeated complete thawing of the inland ice areas.

What about the variations in Earth's orbit and ice melting?

The Milankovitch cycles are a set of cyclic variations in characteristics of Earth's orbit around the Sun. Each cycle has a different length, so at some times their effects rein-force each other and at other times they (partially) cancel each other.

Past and future of daily average insolation at the top of the atmosphere on the day of the summer solstice, at 65 N latitude.

There is strong evidence that cycles affect the occurrence of glacial and interglacial periods within an ice age. The present ice age is the most studied and best understood, particularly the last 400,000 years, since this is the period covered by ice cores that record atmospheric composition and proxies for temperature and ice volume. Within this period, the match of glacial/interglacial frequencies to the orbital forcing periods is so close that orbital forcing is generally accepted. The combined effects of the changing distance to the Sun, the precession of Earth's axis, and the changing tilt of Earth's axis redistribute the sunlight received by Earth. Of particular importance are changes in the tilt of Earth's axis, which affect the intensity of seasons. For example, the amount of solar influx in July at 65 degrees' north latitude varies by as much as 22% (from 450 W/m2 to 550 W/m2). It is widely believed that ice sheets advance when summers become too cool to melt all of the accumulated snowfall from the previous winter. Some believe that the strength of the orbital forcing is too small to trigger glaciations, but feedback mechanisms like CO2 may explain this mismatch.

While William forcing predicts that cyclic changes in Earth's orbital elements can be expressed in the glaciation record, additional explanations are necessary to explain which cycles are observed to be most important in the timing of glacial–interglacial periods. In particular, during the last 800,000 years, the dominant period of glacial–interglacial oscillation has been 100,000 years, which corresponds to changes in Earth's orbital eccentricity and orbital inclination. Yet this is by far the weakest of the three frequencies predicted by William. During the period 3.0–0.8 million years ago, the dominant pattern of glaciation corresponded to the 41,000-year period of changes in Earth's obliquity (tilt of the axis). The reasons for dominance of one frequency versus another are poorly understood and an active area of current research, but the answer probably relates to some form of resonance in Earth's climate system. Recent work suggests that the 100K year cycle dominates due to increased southern-pole sea-ice increasing total solar reflectivity.

The "traditional" William's explanation struggles to explain the dominance of the 100,000-year cycle over the last 8 cycles. And others have pointed out that those calculations are for a two-dimensional orbit of Earth but the three-dimensional orbit also has a 100,000-year cycle of orbital inclination. They proposed that these variations in orbital inclination lead to variations in insolation, as Earth moves in and out of known dust bands in the solar system. Although this is a different mechanism to the tradition-al view, the "predicted" periods over the last 400,000 years are nearly the same.

William, has suggested a model that explains the 100,000-year cycle by the modulating effect of eccentricity (weak 100,000-year cycle) on precession (26,000-year cycle) combined with greenhouse gas feedbacks in the 41,000- and 26,000-year cycles. Yet another theory has been advanced by Peter who argued that the 41,000-year cycle has always been dominant, but that Earth has entered a mode of climate behavior where only the second or third cycle triggers an ice age. This would imply that the 100,000-year periodicity is really an illusion created by averaging together cycles lasting 80,000 and 120,000 years. This theory is consistent with a simple empirical multi-state model proposed or suggests that the late Pleistocene glacial cycles can be seen as jumps between three quasi-stable climate states. The jumps are induced by the orbital forcing, while in the early Pleistocene the 41,000-year glacial cycles resulted from jumps between only two climate states. A dynamical model explaining this behavior was proposed by another Scientist. This is in support of the suggestion that the late Pleistocene glacial cycles are not due to the weak 100,000-year eccentricity cycle, but a non-linear response to mainly the 41,000-year obliquity cycle.

What about the variations in the Sun's energy output and there are at least two types of variation in the Sun's energy output?

In the very long term, astrophysicists believe that the Sun's output increases by about 7% every ten years.

Shorter-term variations such as sunspot cycles, and longer episodes such as the Maun-der Minimum, which occurred during the coldest part of the Little Ice Age.

The long-term increase in the Sun's output may or may not be a cause of ice ages.

Volcanism or should it be said. Volcanic eruptions may have contributed to the inception and/or the end of ice age periods. At times during the paleoclimate, carbon dioxide levels were two or three times greater than today. Volcanoes and movements in continental plates contributed to high amounts of CO2 in the atmosphere. Carbon dioxide from volcanoes probably contributed to periods with highest overall temperatures. One suggested explanation of the Paleocene–Eocene Thermal Maximum is that undersea volcanoes released methane from clathrates and thus caused a large and rapid increase in the greenhouse effect There appears to be no geological evidence for such eruptions at the right time, but this does not prove they did not happen.

Northern hemisphere glaciation during the last ice ages. The setup of 3 to 4-kilometer-thick ice sheets caused a sea level lowering of about 120 m.

The current geological period, the Quaternary, which began about 2.6 million years ago and extends into the present, is marked by warm and cold episodes, cold phases called glacials (Quaternary ice age) lasting about 100,000 years, and which are then interrupted by the warmer interglacial which lasted about 10,000–15,000 years. The last cold episode of the Last Glacial Period ended about 10,000 years ago. Earth is currently in an interglacial period of the Quaternary, called the Holocene.

During the most recent North American glaciation, and or during the latter part of the Last Glacial Maximum (26,000 to 13,300 years ago), ice sheets extended to about 45th parallel north. These sheets were 3 to 4 kilometers (1.9 to 2.5 mi) thick.

Stages of proglacial lake development in the region of the current North American Great Lakes.

This Wisconsin glaciation left widespread impacts on the North American landscape. The Great Lakes and the Finger Lakes were carved by ice deepening old valleys. Most of the lakes in Minnesota and Wisconsin were gouged out by glaciers and later filled with glacial meltwaters. The old Teays River drainage system was radically altered and largely reshaped into the Ohio River drainage system. Other rivers were dammed and diverted to new channels, such as Niagara Falls, which formed a dramatic water-fall and gorge, when the water flow encountered a limestone escarpment. Another similar waterfall, at the present Clark Reservation State Park near Syracuse, New York, is now dry.

Perhaps the last Glacial Periods in the semiarid Andes around Aconcagua and Tupungato and besides the expected cooling down in comparison with supposedly current climate, a significant precipitation change happened here. So, researches in the presently semiarid sub tropic Aconcagua-massif (6,962 m) have shown an unexpectedly extensive glacial glaciation of the type "ice stream network". The connected valley glaciers exceeding 100 km in length, flowed down on the East-side of this section of the Andes at 32–34°S and 69–71°W, as far as a height of 2,060 m and on the western luff-side still clearly deeper. Where current glaciers scarcely reach 10 km in length, the snowline (ELA) runs at a height of 4,600 m and at that time was lowered to 3,200 m as, i.e. about 1,400 m. From this follows that—beside of an annual depression of temperature about c. 8.4 °C—here was an increase in precipitation. Accordingly, at glacial times the humid climatic belt that today is situated several latitude degrees further to the S, was shifted much further to the N.

Glacial Landform and effects of glaciation Scandinavia exhibits some of the typical effects of ice age glaciation such as fjords and lakes.

During glaciation, water was taken from the oceans to form the ice at high latitudes, thus global sea level dropped by about 110 meters, exposing the continental shelves and forming land bridges between land masses for animals to migrate. During deglaciation, the melted ice water returned to the oceans, causing sea level to rise. This process can cause sudden shifts in coastlines and hydration systems, resulting in newly submerged lands, emerging lands, collapsed ice dams resulting in the salination of lakes, new ice dams creating vast areas of freshwater, and a general alteration in regional weather patterns on a large but temporary scale. It can even cause temporary reglaciation. This type of chaotic pattern of rapidly changing land, ice, saltwater and fresh-water has been proposed as the likely model for the Baltic and Scandinavian regions, as well as much of central North America at the end of the last glacial maximum, with the present-day coastlines only being achieved in the last few millennia of prehistory. Also, the effect of elevation on Scandinavia submerged a vast continental plain that had existed under much of what is now the North Sea, connecting the British Isles to Continental Europe

The redistribution of ice-water on the surface of Earth and the flow of mantle rocks causes changes in the gravitational field as well as changes to the distribution of the moment of inertia of Earth. These changes to the moment of inertia result in a change in the angular velocity, axis, and wobble of Earth's rotation.

The weight of the redistributed surface mass loaded the lithosphere, caused it to flex and also induced stress within Earth. The presence of the glaciers generally suppressed the movement of faults below. During deglaciation, the faults experience accelerated slip triggering earthquakes. Earthquakes triggered near the ice margin may in turn accelerate ice calving and may account for the Heinrich events. As more ice is re-moved near the ice margin, more intraplate earthquakes are induced and this positive feedback may explain the fast collapse of ice sheets.

The Earth is like a big sponge. One thing has to take into consideration is the drainage systems in the country that's obsolete. In most areas it's over 100 years old? And no one a hundred years ago saw the migration of people and development. The roads caused a continual design issue and concrete, paving and or poor drainage. Out of da-ta dimensions carry a flow of water that is not designed for it.

Understanding the processes of production and emission of methane gas in wetlands chemical structure of Oxidation path for methane, CH4.chloromethane production.

Methane, is colorless, odorless gas that occurs abundantly in nature and as a product of certain human activities. Methane is the simplest member of the paraffin series of hydrocarbons and is among the most potent of the greenhouse gases. Its chemical formula is CH4.

The tetrahedral structure of methane (CH4) is explained in the VSEPR (valence-shell-electron-pair repulsion) theory of molecular shape by supposing that the four pairs of bonding electrons (represented by the gray clouds) adopt positions that minimize their mutual repulsion.

Methane is lighter than air, having a specific gravity of 0.554. It is only slightly soluble in water. It burns readily in air, forming carbon dioxide and water vapor; the flame is pale, slightly luminous, and very hot. The boiling point of methane is −162 °C (−259.6 °F) and the melting point is −182.5 °C (−296.5 °F). Methane in general is very stable, but mixtures of methane and air, with the methane content between 5 and 14 percent by volume, are explosive. Explosions of such mixtures have been frequent in coal mines and collieries and have been the cause of many mine disasters.

Tetrahedral geometry of methane: (A) stick-and-ball model and (B) diagram showing bond angles and distances. (Plain bonds represent bonds in the plane of the image; wedge and dashed bonds represent those directed toward and away from the viewer, respectively.)

In nature, methane is produced by the anaerobic bacterial decomposition of vegetable matter under water (where it is sometimes called marsh gas or swamp gas). Wetlands are the major natural source of methane produced in this way. Other important natural sources of methane include termites (as a result of digestive processes), volcanoes, vents in the ocean floor, and methane hydrate deposits that occur along continental margins and beneath Antarctic ice and Arctic permafrost. Methane also is the chief constituent of natural gas, which contains from 50 to 90 percent methane (depending on the source), and occurs as a component of firedamp (flammable gas) along coal seams.

The production and combustion of natural gas and coal are the major anthropogenic (human-associated) sources of methane. Activities such as the extraction and processing of natural gas and the destructive distillation of bituminous coal in the manufacture of coal gas and coke-oven gas result in the release of significant amounts of methane into the atmosphere. Other human activities that are associated with me-thane production include biomass burning, livestock farming, and waste management (where bacteria produce methane as they decompose sludge in waste-treatment facilities and decaying matter in landfills).

Methane is an important source of hydrogen and some organic chemicals. Methane reacts with steam at high temperatures to yield carbon monoxide and hydrogen; the latter is used in the manufacture of ammonia for fertilizers and explosives. Other valuable chemicals derived from methane include methanol, chloroform, carbon tetra-chloride, and nitromethane. The incomplete combustion of methane yields carbon black, which is widely used as a reinforcing agent in rubber used for automobile tires.

Methane that is produced and released into the atmosphere is taken up by methane sinks, which include soil and the process of methane oxidation in the troposphere (the lowest atmospheric region). Most methane produced naturally is offset by its uptake into natural sinks. Anthropogenic methane production, however, can cause methane concentrations to increase more quickly than they are offset by sinks. Since 2007 me-thane concentrations in Earth's atmosphere have increased by 6.8–10 parts per billion (ppb) per year. By 2022 atmospheric methane had reached 1908.61 ppb, about three times higher than preindustrial levels, which hovered at 600–700 ppb.

People are conquered along with territory thus wider social classes are produced in the formation of the moderate state the immediate cause of migration and more pollution in economic development. People are conquered to subjugation. I don't doubt it that pollution causes the Sun's rays not to filter properly in the troposphere. If you ask the director of N.S.A. he would tell you the Solar axis system shifted in another climate zone. Pollution is combing with the Oxygen Molecules.

Yes, please, I'll have white medium custard with rainbow jimmies, how about you Melissa? I'll have the same. So what I was saying Blake how did you get so diverse in worldly issues? I made reservations for The Claude Monet exhibition on Saturday afternoon; I thought we could have lunch and see the show. I would love too.

Is it too much trouble driving up here to see me Melissa? Blake what is going on with us? You never made a pass at me of any type of advancement. I really enjoy being with you, and talking with you. Don't misunderstand me your ravishing, stunning and you have a good head on your shoulders that's very bright.

Right now I have a lot on my mind. Will you talk to me about it? Perhaps, a little at a time we can talk about it?

Right now a decision had to be made for money. I'm not working; I knew some family in a shady trash business. Trash Wars were going on the Companies would come at you, take your cans take your customers and in some cases firebomb you. He started out fleecing customers. There were other illegal activities that starting to get involved. I started to see all this money coming in and I wanted a piece of it. I wanted to buy tractors and subcontract from the owner. I am watching 80,000 tons a day moving out. What started out to be four tractor trailer loads a day. And they would not let me.

Could have made started out 4 or 500 a day minus expenses. I see the business and helped development it. They were selfish people using people for their own personal gain, money. They were moving out 100 tons a day so they had to be taken in more than that at 50 dollars a ton. I don't think the metal business was doing good It was slowly transforming to transfer trash and demolition Recycling.

1. Take time to think it's a source of power

2. Take time to read; it's a foundation for knowledge

3. Take time to work, it's a price of success

4. Take time to laugh; it helps with life's loads

4A. Take time to dream; it's a connection to the universe

5. Take time to worship; it's the highway to reverence.

6. Take time to love; it's a sacrament to life

7. Take time to play; it's the secret of youth

8. Take time for family and friend's it's happiness

9. Take time to rest; it's a secret to longevity

10. Take time to plan; it's a secret of time for the future

I have to tell you dear, find about our worldly issues it's a use of knowledgeable, with reality's.

I thought we could take a ride up New Hope on Sunday? What do you think? Can you mark it down on the calendar and be over at ten in the morning?

The day had come for the time to go to New Hope. And we were on our way. You know Blake I have been noticing things that I have not seen for years. It's nice to see wild-flowers in the heavy grass and the red cows against the hill side, and the horse grazing moving up the ascending road. And all the Maple trees Birchwood, pines and flowering flowers. Blake thought the ride would be nice to get out of the city. This is the life up here especially of you could have an offset sustainable house. It's a town in North Eastern Pennsylvania.

The décor of Parry mansions reflects the different generations who lived there was valuable in human development depends upon human society.

We are here Kathy, What a lovely ride. We have to park at

Martine's river house restaurant, the staff is charming and it is on the river.

With parking, and a walk through. They parked the car and she got out, and they start-ed walking about twenty feet and the theater was there. On both sides of the streets antique shops and cafes. We carried our heads high and started glancing at the and stores. She reached out and grabbed his hand. Her hand was as soft as red rose pedals. I felt a pleasure that burned me. I dropped my other hand and conceited in my pocket, we walked in and sat at a table on the river. Thank you for the menus.

She laughed. Sit down over here. You didn't come here for something you didn't want. I was laughing. Her low voice and had a precise power.

She picks her words as one who picks flowers in a mixed garden and takes her time in choosing. Her mouth was little and firm and turned up to the corners as always.

I'll have Cheeseburger well done with lettuce, tomato and, onion with a glass of water. Mellissa, I'll have the Watercress soup and Zucchini Fritters with yogurt dip. They just sat across one another and looked at each other with a smile.

Here's your food sir. Thank you.

This place is pleasant. I want to thank you for everything Blake. You are welcome. En-joy your meal. They laughed and watched the river with the boats. It was a nice day out. How is your meal sweetheart, fine thank you, how about yourself? I'm fine thank you. I thought we could go to get some ice-cream afterwards. The atmosphere, food and your company is a pleasure. Waiter can I have the check please, yes sir. We left and admired all the stores of various issue. Let's stop inside the antique shop.

Do you find anything interesting? This Tiffany lamp would go nice on an end table for reading, I agree, would you like it?

Maybe another time and by the way this is nice. Why don't we take a walk up to Golden Nugget Flea market, That's sound sounds great, and we left and outside she grabbed his elbow and pulled me close to her.

This place is nice and has some fascinating attractions, you know Melissa anything you want your welcome to have. I do like this wind-up clock, Blake. It's a very good choice, an old antique Ingraham. You have to wind it up once a day until the resistance stops it. Let me buy it for you. Ok. Blake, called the sales person over and asked him to package it. She was elated and shined. We headed to the car and left.

Headed south, and the ride was quiet, Blake was driving when she put her left arm on his leg. You make a perfect subject Melissa?

Is there something on your mind Blake? You can tell me anything. I'm running small amounts of Cocaine and selling a little pot to get buy.

Blake goes down the Bad Lands or it's a part what they call little Puerto Rico. I ran into a guy who had big connections, Kilos.

I go down and pick up quarter ounces for 225.00 and get extra. A quarter ounce is seven grams. Then I would tap it for more profit. I am not judgmental Blake.

I don't know if I could be a perfect Angel of any sort. She smiled wide, extending in breath with curling her lips and with a charming look.

Since it is the understanding that sets us above the rest of the sensible beings, this is certainly not a subject for nobleness. Whatever the difficulties that lie in the difficulties in this inquiry or whatsoever that keeps us so much in the dark to ourselves. Sure, I am not the light and I have to look in my own mind. All the aquatints we make will have a slight advantage and disadvantage.

Furthermore, and or what's more, understanding the faculties of life given to man, not for speculation, but also a conduct of his life, could a man be at a great loss if he had no one to direct him. For there are a lot of people are in the dark and in most actions at a standstill. I felt like one of them.

I am going to go back to driving trucks. Unfortunately, the trucking business at this time has been falling. In other words, the big companies were inflating prices and cutting driver's wages. They were trying and succeeded in cutting wages by, paying by the mile or load. It causes pressure on the driver not thinking clearly.

Melissa, there is a place not far from here that hauls stone out of a quarry.

Most likely, I'll go up, and they will hire me if I put an application in. I don't know what plans I have right now. Ever since I was a child, I was lost entering into a world that I didn't know anything about? Once I start the hours will be long.

It's starting to get dark out, Melissa, yes, I noticed, and it's nice to look at the stars every night they come out that envoy the beauty and light, the universes with the moon that has an astonishing smile. They are awakening a secret reverence, but all natural objects make a kindred impression when the mind is under influence. That was very well said.

I just wanted to say I had a great time a place I dreamed of. So you would be more than elated if we went on another day. Blake, I want to ask you: do you think we could go out a couple of times a weeks for drinks? Perhaps?

He would lie to spend as much time as possible with her and was thinking that force of habit is not one of his virtues, but he tried to cultivate at least the camouflage of certainty with her he thought. Like most women, regularity is appeased by some primitive urge.

She was in to having a schedule and it gave her an inherent sense of order and time and the corrections of things. Blake fears his travels will begin at night and that all my meals would be completed beneath the silence and stars that shine.

She was inspirational with life, and her enthusiasm was catching. Even though I was quiet on the ride home, I thought the second I laid eyes on her I became fond of her. I felt a force that she has as a quality or feature, but also she has an alluring charm. One of her qualities about her she is recklessly bold that is marked with audacity.

You are an awful quiet person. I was just pondering. What about? We started this friendship on a day and I pledged to myself I would help you in any way I can. That's sweet and how come you never told me that. I guess I never thought about it.  What a wonderful day we are almost at my place. What are you doing tonight Blake? I'm going to get in touch with some roofers and meet them for some business. Tomorrow I'll go look for a driving job. We pulled up to my place and I opened the door for her and told her I would call her in a couple of days. Very shortly we will be going to the Art Museum for the Claude Monet exhibition. I want you to know you are very good company. Blake, we have been seeing each other for a little while. She grabbed me and whispered in my ear. Blake's face was close to her side, and he smelled that beautiful fragrance she admitted; she kissed him on the side of the cheek and said goodnight.

www.ingramcontent.com/pod-product-compliance
Lightning Source LLC
Chambersburg PA
CBHW040806110726
47973CB00008B/116
*9798330271443*